"G Street Lion is a moving celebration of self-discovery and struggle. Its primary message is hugely timely: we can, indeed, become the best that our dreams promise."
— MINDY THOMPSON FULLILOVE, MD, MS,
PROFESSOR OF CLINICAL PSYCHIATRY, AUTHOR, ROOT SHOCK

"Since 1943, the Jackie Robinson Family YMCA has served kids and families in San Diego County's most critical community. G Street Lion tells the story of how one of those kids has made an impact near and far because so many did the same throughout his life."
— MICHAEL BRUNKER,
EXECUTIVE DIRECTOR, JACKIE ROBINSON FAMILY YMCA

"This powerful story will resonate with anyone who cheers for the underdog or dares to see the potential in humble beginnings."
— RUDOLPH A. JOHNSON, III,
PRESIDENT AND CEO, NEIGHBORHOOD HOUSE ASSOCIATION

"G Street Lion is one of those transformative works that reminds us all that great and good things often come from terrible adversity."
— ROBERT E. FULLILOVE, EdD, MS,
ASSOCIATE DEAN, COLUMBIA UNIVERSITY

"G Street Lion reminds us that 'What does not destroy you will only make you stronger.'"
— REV. HAROLD R. JOLLEY, M.DIV.,
PASTOR-TEACHER, SECOND MACEDONIA BAPTIST CHURCH, PHILADELPHIA

"Rare is the student that makes an educator stop and take notice...LaMar was remarkable in third grade. LaMar was the first student, in my tenure as an elementary school counselor, who made a difference in my life!"
— PAM PERRY SMAL,
COUNSELOR (K-12) SAN DIEGO UNIFIED SCHOOL DISTRICT, RETIRED

G STREET
Lion
STALKING A DREAM

LaMar Hasbrouck, MD
Foreword by Reed V. Tuckson, MD

G STREET LION
STALKING A DREAM

iUniverse books may be ordered through booksellers or by contacting:

iUniverse
1663 Liberty Drive
Bloomington, IN 47403
www.iuniverse.com
1-800-Authors (1-800-288-4677)

ISBN: 978-1-4917-9254-4 (sc)
ISBN: 978-1-4917-9256-8 (hc)
ISBN: 978-1-4917-9255-1 (e)

Print information available on the last page.

iUniverse rev. date: 05/27/2016

For my remarkable daughters, Baele, Maysa, and Lalah, who inspire me daily; for my sister who gave up much of her childhood to take care of "her boys"; for my mother and secret weapon; and in loving memory of Mrs. Mae Francis Roberts, who devoted her life to saving young people in my neighborhood.

There are no mistakes or failures, only lessons.

—Denis Waitley

Contents

PART 4
WHITE-COAT MIND-SET

PART 5
MISSION-DRIVEN

Foreword

The phrase "role model" gets used so often that sometimes it loses its significance. However, some lives really are significant in their potential to cause other people to try to reach the fullest dimensions of their own humanness. I am fortunate to travel extensively across our great nation and speak with many people of different races, cultures, genders, ages, and socioeconomic classes. More often than not, I am left with the clear sense that people are simultaneously greatly frustrated with their lives and the world around them and eager to capture the bright lights and shining beacons of hope that burst in like the dawn. It is important for all of us to experience examples of people who have learned how to live lives of greater purpose and transcendent value. This is especially true for people of color and other disenfranchised people.

As the former president of the Charles R. Drew University of Medicine and Science, located in South Central Los Angeles, I had the privilege of supporting a faculty that was dedicated to training the next generation of health professionals who were committed to meeting the health needs of traditionally underserved communities. The young people who were attracted to our school self-selected themselves as being committed to the highest ideals of the healing professions. Something about their life experiences to that point in their young lives; something about the way they were nurtured by their families and communities; something in their unique DNA of spirit and consciousness; something led them to their profession and the pursuit of that profession in South Central Los Angeles.

One day, out of these beacons of light stepped boldly, confidently, beautifully, and articulately a young student by the name of LaMar Hasbrouck. LaMar felt the need for a mentor, so why not the president of the university? Thus began my almost twenty-year witness to a remarkable young man's journey to discovering himself as a fully realized black man; as a proud American man; as a husband and father; and as an especially effective physician who has kept faith with the timeless ideals of his profession.

It has been my privilege to have experienced LaMar as a mentee, collaborator, and now as a friend, and even, sometimes, as *his* student. Reading this book, I now better understand that my young student's passions were strongly shaped by his previous experiences and, equally important, by his reactions to those experiences. If we just take the time, we can learn so much by paying attention to other people's lives. LaMar's story helps me to understand better that passion and compassion are important qualities that must be constantly nurtured by the sensitive soul. However, leaders, as Dr. Hasbrouck demonstrates, must be prepared to undertake the discipline required to master the skills and expertise necessary to translate passion into meaningful action. It is my great hope that the potential for leadership that lies undiscovered and unrewarded in so many of our children will, in at least a few cases, be unlocked by exposure to LaMar's story.

What may not come through on the printed page is that Dr. Hasbrouck, in addition to being an excellent professional and a man of substance, has also been blessed to live a pretty cool life. Personable, articulate, and enthusiastic, he exhibits that natural swagger that comes with the confidence of the talented athlete. A successful football player at a challenging college program, LaMar was able to use the challenges presented on the practice and playing field as key training grounds for rounding out his development as a man. The principles embodied in the aspirations of the scholar-athlete concept came to fruition in LaMar's life. It is an unfortunate reality that still, today, so many young students need to be reminded that you can be smart, bookish, athletically accomplished, dress sharp, and maintain your cool as a man and your integrity as a man of color.

If America is to continue its journey to realizing its fullest potential, it needs to nurture and develop thousands more LaMars. They need to come from all of America's communities, but especially, they need to come from communities of color and other disadvantaged populations. These new leaders need to understand that today's world has little interest in excuses but needs people who are prepared to overcome whatever obstacles are placed in their path. LaMar Hasbrouck's story is important and will be inspiring to many. Having enjoyed the privilege of watching him grow and fulfill his dreams, his story makes me hunger to applaud the thousands of others like him who are just waiting to emerge.

It is my hope that this story will encourage all those young people who need examples of success to help push them along their way. That it will embolden parents as they confront the difficult challenges of raising children in this increasingly complex world, and that it will encourage people who have access to wealth and resources to redouble their efforts to extend a helping hand to those individuals and institutions that just need a small break at just the right time.

As exciting as Dr. Hasbrouck's journey has been, I am even more enthusiastic about the person that he is yet to become. I certainly plan on going along for that ride as well. In the meantime, let's find, nurture, and celebrate many more like him!

Reed V. Tuckson, MD
Managing Director
Tuckson Health Connections

Preface

A young man waited to introduce himself to me after a talk I gave at Morehouse College. The historically black college is located in Atlanta, but he was enrolled at Stanford University in California. He was at Morehouse on an exchange program. It turned out that he was from my hometown of San Diego, California.

He told me that our backgrounds were similar and said he wanted to be like me. "Doctor Hasbrouck, I want to do what you're doing. I plan to attend medical school and have a career just like you."

Needless to say, I was flattered. Aware of the power of mentoring, I always made it my practice to give my contact information whenever I gave a talk to young people. So when this aspiring medical student from my hometown asked if he could interview me for his class project, I agreed. How could I refuse?

We scheduled the interview a few weeks later. He appeared promptly at my office on that day with a notepad and a small tape recorder, and he asked me all of the usual questions: How long have you been at your job? Where did you attend school? Who were your mentors? What made you choose medicine as a career?

Then he asked me an odd question. "If you were an animal, what kind of animal would you be?" Although I was curious to know why he had asked such an unusual question, I immediately answered, "A lion."

When he asked me to explain, I reflected on my life's path. I told him that a lion is successful at catching his prey because of his approach. He waits patiently. Sizing up his target, he plans out the best route to attack. After studying his target long and hard, he moves in slowly, taking measured steps, stalking. Each step is a carefully planned one. Using the tall grass as cover, he draws nearer, undetected. When he comes within striking distance, he leaps out from the tall grass and chases his target. Before the intended prey is aware, it is pounced upon and caught. The poor animal never saw the lion coming.

Acknowledgments

I am indebted to Tom Shanahan for his article titled "Healthy Values" that appeared in the *San Diego Union-Tribune* on November 23, 2001. The article written about me caught the eye of Paul, a retired book editor who, together with Tom, convinced me to embark on this project. I owe an immeasurable debt of gratitude to my friend and book coach, Sheryl Mallory-Johnson, who reviewed numerous drafts, provided detailed critique, and pressed me to find my authentic voice. Thanks also to Pam Perry-Smal for her copy editing and relentless enthusiastic support. She's known me just about my entire life and still finds my story interesting. Imagine that. Thank you to Holly Andersen for throwing me a lifeline when I was at my lowest. It's so important to have someone believe in you when you doubt yourself. She did at a critical time in my life trajectory. And to the many mentors and friends who have graciously provided me with coaching for my professional, personal, spiritual, and intellectual growth—thank you. This list includes Ed Wilson, Bob Fullilove, Mindy Fullilove, Patricia Morgan, Reed V. Tuckson, Rudolph A. Johnson III, Dexter Jones, Willie Parker, Harold Jolley, and others. Finally, I am grateful for the support of my immediate and extended family during this creative process.

Introduction: At My Lowest

Landing in New York City on a cool East Coast day, I brought my California glow and laid-back attitude with me. I was physically exhausted from finishing up medical school, attending two graduation ceremonies, the senior banquet, and packing, but I was optimistic to start a new chapter in my life. Officially I was still in training, but for the first time in my life, I wore the title "doctor." I had every reason to be hopeful.

My first order of business was to stop by the housing office for the keys to my high-rise apartment. Right off, my dream began to unravel. The manager, a short Italian woman, met me in her office.

"Yes, Doctor. I have your keys right here. I'm just going to need your first month's rent and security deposit. That comes to $1,250."

That was not the answer I expected. I assumed my rent would come directly out of my paycheck. I fully expected to grab my key and move into my studio, I explained. She nodded and smiled agreeably.

"Yes, Doctor. Only rent deduction won't begin until after your first paycheck," she said with a persistent smile.

My heart sunk into my stomach because that meant we had a problem. There was $236 in my pocket, and that was all I had. Defeated and a little embarrassed, I wondered if I was prepared for this leg of my journey. Hoping that my lack of cash wasn't an omen for more bad news, I left her office and went to the hospital laundry department to pick up my salmon-colored scrubs. "Doctor LaMar

Hasbrouck, Internal Medicine," the white labels fixed to my three spanking-new pairs of scrubs read. I took it as a sign that I was indeed in the place I belonged.

With that reassurance, I began making frantic phone calls to California. I called my parents, my grandparents, and Smitty. It was an all-out family SOS. My studio apartment, equipped with newish appliances, beautiful hardwoods, and a gorgeous view, was without a single piece of furniture. Other than the four duffle bags, a boom box, a nineteen-inch Sony Trinitron TV, several boxes of books, and an exercise mat that I brought from home, the place was empty. That mat became my bed for the first few weeks until my relief package arrived.

Surviving on plantains, yellow rice, beans, and gravy, I pushed through orientation week. Lectures and advanced life-saving courses took up most of my days. In the evenings, I spent a lot of my time looking out of my window of the Helmsley Medical Towers, twenty-seven stories above the world, beyond the bustling traffic on the FDR Drive, out at the East River.

Wow! I'm here in the Big Apple. Had I slipped into the program undetected? At every turn, I began to imagine that certain tap on my shoulder, someone pulling me aside, hearing those dreaded words: "You don't belong here. There was an error. Pack up and get going."

My days were long and tedious; my nights dragged on even longer. Missing home terribly, I longed for my old girlfriend, the one I had broken up with just months before the move. I longed to lay up with my new girlfriend, the one I had just begun to grow so fond of before leaving California. Desperate to talk to someone, I called her constantly, bending her ear for hours at a time. I found myself in relative isolation for the first time in a long time. Often, I lay in bed, listening to music on my boom box or the sound of my heartbeat above the steady commotion of the city sounds.

The isolation eventually took its toll on me. It became apparent when one day while walking down the street, past my favorite deli, I leaped onto a man's back. Don't ask me what compelled me to do it. I recognized him as a third-year surgical resident whom I had met briefly at a black medical student function at Cornell University. He seemed like good people. But that in no way gave me the right to sneak up on him as if he was my best friend from the old neighborhood. The brother was clean-cut, with a slender, athletic build like mine but taller. He must have thought a monkey landed on his back.

"What's up, man?" he said sharply with a bewildered look on his face, shrugging me off his back. "You shouldn't sneak up on someone like that," he protested.

His protest sounded more like a threat. He had every right to threaten me, to kick my ass if he pleased. I didn't say anything while he stared me down, his face as puzzled as mine. *What am I doing?* I thought. *Am I losing it? I barely know this guy. Why would I sneak up on him and jump on his back like his kid brother?* Unable to explain my spontaneous actions, I avoided eye contact, sank back, and disappeared into the crowd. *I'm losing it,* I thought.

My first assignment as a real medical doctor was to the sixteenth floor of the medical towers, the inpatient medical ward. I inherited a roster of fifteen patients that I didn't know from Adam, but I was responsible for every one of them. With overnight call looming every fourth night, if I didn't discharge several patients between call nights, my service was at risk of ballooning to twenty or more patients. Too many patients would make daily rounds and patient management nearly impossible. As it was, I was drowning in a sea of patients.

My mornings began at 6:30 a.m. with a report from the post-call intern, who had been on twenty-four-hour call the previous night, to find out how my patients did through the night. A death was not always a bad thing, as odd as that may seem. Some patients, it seemed, were living on borrowed time. Others were long-suffering and caused prolonged grief to their families. Other patients were medically futile, meaning there was nothing medically that we could do for them despite all heroic measures.

In the life of an overwhelmed, sleep-deprived, first-year intern, death could be cause for a silent sigh of relief. Doctors never wished for it. In fact, we did everything within our power to prevent it. Nonetheless, a death meant there was one fewer complicated patient constantly demanding our time and attention. Death became a part of life.

After receiving the report on what happened overnight, I started my pre-rounds, which included looking in on every patient and reviewing their information, things like vital signs, fluid intake, urine outflow, and doing a quick, focused examination. After finishing, I shadowed my resident, a second- or third-year doctor in the program, dragging myself from room to room.

Rob and I walked into Mrs. Brenner's room; she was an elderly white woman with breast cancer. As we entered, she sat feebly in bed, staring at me as if I had the answer to all that ailed her. If only I did. I put on a pretend smile, opened her chart, and said, "Good morning, Mrs. Brenner. How are you feeling today?" My mind felt like a bloated sponge, unable to soak up another ounce of information as the patient described her list of concerns. Although her lips were moving, her words couldn't penetrate the thickness of my fatigue. Quiet as kept, I secretly wished I was the one lying in bed all day, resting, awaiting a team of caring people to come with the answers to my questions.

I turned to Rob and said, "She's tolerating the chemo all right." At least that's what it looked like to me. She was receiving her second cycle of chemotherapy, and her immune system had taken a beating, which made her vulnerable to infections. On top of that, she was anemic and required occasional blood transfusions. But she was alive, and most of her critical lab values seemed to be holding steady. As the most inexperienced doctor in the room, I spoke out just to establish myself as a credible member of the medical team, not so much because I had an earthshaking opinion about her course of care.

"Mrs. Brenner, so far everything is going according to plan. It's too early to know anything more definitive at this point. We'll just take it one day at a time. Do you have any questions for us?" Rob added. In his second year of the training program, Rob was a tall, thin, white boy with a stern, almost emotionless face. He was all business and seldom cracked a smile or shared a light moment.

No sooner had we left Mrs. Brenner's room than Rob started in on me with the questions, questions that he knew I couldn't answer.

This constant questioning, or testing, by more senior physicians, was part teaching and part reinforcing their superior knowledge. It was the age-old process of roundsmanship, or being socialized into the profession of medicine. When it occurred within a group of doctors, during walking rounds with the attending physicians, for example, it felt like we were being pimped. So that's what we called it: being pimped.

"Doctor Hasbrouck, can you tell me the most common organisms that cause community-acquired pneumonia among smokers?" the senior physician in charge of the medical service for that month said.

Heck if I know. I'm just trying to get my work done so I can go home at a reasonable hour tonight. But silence is not acceptable when you're being pimped.

"Uh, strep pneumonia," I replied sheepishly before a long pause.

"Streptococcus pneumonia, B. catarrhalis, and Haemophilus influenza," he corrected.

"Oh yeah, right," I said, trying to save face. *At least I got one out of three of them bad boys right. Not bad.*

When all the rounding ended, the real work began. Managing fifteen patients was a hell of a lot for any intern. My hands aching, my eyes half-closed, and the clock my enemy, I found myself unable to complete the required daily progress notes on all of my patients, despite working late into the evening. The number of tasks that I had to juggle for each of my patients seemed to snow me under. Like a goldfish in a blender, every day was equal to swimming the span of the Atlantic Ocean, with weak arms, tired legs, and a weary mind. I had a little kick left in me.

It seemed like the folks from the top medical schools like Brown University, the University of California at San Francisco, and Michigan had breezed across the rough waters and were waiting for me to catch up. I would drown before touching dry land. Of this, I was sure. If my body wasn't swimming, my head certainly was from countless tasks. Sometimes I was able to fudge a little and write a quick progress note in a few charts the next morning and backdate them. Other times, I completely screwed up.

My turn finally came to take call. I sprung out of bed, dressed, and left my apartment with nervous anticipation as adrenaline-rich blood rushed to my head. Strutting confidently down the corridors, I began the day's grind, sporting my hospital scrubs for the first time with my crisp, white coat pockets bulging with small reference books that would coach me through the night.

The morning flew by as my long list of slave duties blended right into a late lunch of beans and rice. Before no time at all, early evening was upon me, and my fellow interns began signing out their patients to me. They explained their patient lists, pointing out the unstable ones to watch and the lab values I needed to monitor overnight.

"Mrs. Witkow is here for an elective procedure to have an aneurysm clipped. She is stable, nothing to do for her. You need to watch Mr. Hamburg though," my fellow intern instructed.

"What's his deal?" I confidently replied, as if I could handle it no matter what.

"He's an eighty-five-year-old admitted with suspected endocarditis. If he spikes a fever over 101.3, you need to be sure to take blood and urine cultures. Oh, and watch his blood pressure. He tends to bottom out," the intern reported.

One after another, each intern lined up to go over their list of ten to fifteen patients with me and hand me their cheat sheets, until I was left holding patient lists for all three interns. Including my own, this accounted for every patient on the ward, about fifty in all. Pretending to have it all under control, I sat at the nurses' station writing a to-do list for the night. Tucking in fifty patients, chasing lab results, and being available when the nurses needed me was the least of my worries. Running down to the ER to admit new patients to add to my ever-expanding list was the thing I dreaded most.

Things were quiet at the nurses' station except for the usual background noise of flipping through charts, the chatter of nurses answering phone calls, and nurses directing visiting family members to the rooms of their loved ones. Busy with checking lab values at the computer and finishing up progress notes, I made small talk with a fresh shift of nurses who would become my best friends overnight.

It was a necessary practice to seal the intern-nurse covenant. Treat the nurses with respect and kindness, and they would keep your butt out of hot water and allow you to get a few winks of sleep, if possible. Act like a pompous know-it-all, and they'd let you crash and burn.

Not more than an hour into my shift, I stood up to return a chart and felt lightheaded. Without warning, I collapsed, right in the middle of the nursing station.

"Are you okay, LaMar? You okay?" my supervising resident, Rob, asked as he stood over me.

"Huh? What? What happened?" I asked in my fog.

"You passed out," he said. "Have you eaten dinner yet?"

I wobbled to a chair, watching the nurses stare at me with concern, or maybe they pitied me. *Dang. I didn't see this coming.*

"Uh, no, not yet," I answered.

"Then you better go grab something."

Feeling as frail as the patients on my lists, not to mention self-conscious, I rested on my feet and walked slowly down a short corridor to the on-call room where I was to sleep that night, assuming I got to sleep at all. I ate the box lunch that was provided for the on-call team, a tuna sandwich, and a ginger ale.

The entire night on-call, I ran around like a chicken with its head cut off. No sooner would I tuck in a new arrival than my pager would go off again.

"Hello, this is Doctor Hasbrouck. I was paged." Each time I said those words, I'd cross my fingers and hold my breath, hoping that the page was a misfire. It wasn't. Instead, it was another new admission for me to work up. Like a sleepwalking mummy, I'd page my resident, meet him in the ER, examine my new admission, and then push the patient down the hallway, up the elevator, and to a permanent bed on the medical unit.

This cycle repeated throughout the night. I may have gotten three hours of interrupted sleep. When the dust settled, I added five new patients to my list. My patient count increased from twelve to seventeen, but at least I survived the night.

The next morning, I left the hospital and limped home. My brain was fried, and my body felt as heavy as lead as I dropped onto my makeshift bed. Too exhausted to dream, I slept in total darkness. I awoke briefly for a foggy dinner and then slipped back into the blackness.

When I awoke the next morning, I felt more tired than when I lay down: awake but not alive, groggy and uninspired. It was as if the previous twenty-four hours extracted the life from me. There was a strange sense of heaviness on me. Not so much on my body but on my mind. With the weight of the day's tasks that lay waiting for me, I felt a sense of impending gloom of a day filled with repetitious, thankless tasks on a never-ending to-do list.

It was an unforgiving cycle with replacement patients added to those that I couldn't discharge fast enough because they were in bad shape. Some had cancer, some breathing problems. Bad livers, bad kidneys, and fever of unknown origin rounded the list. They were like sick puppies, all of them.

Each day was harder and harder for me to endure. Like running in place, I worked my butt off chasing down X-rays and bone scan readings, nuclear tests, and countless lab results. Dispirited, I became reduced to simply going through the motions. Doubts began to creep into my mind about whether or not I was made for this profession.

By Wednesday of my second week on the wards, something inside me gave way. The morning began like any other. I ran behind, so when my team and I walked into the rooms of a few of my patients, it was the first time I had seen them that morning. I crossed my fingers and prayed for stable vital signs and no worsening of their conditions overnight. Who was I fooling? I was in over my head, and this was just more evidence of that.

As I walked with my team, I suddenly felt my eyes glass over. At that very moment, I stepped outside of myself as the world rotated in slow motion, and the crushing cries of self-doubt drowned all sound out. My footsteps dragged slowly. It wasn't long before I fell behind the group as tears slowly rolled down my cheeks. My supervising resident noticed.

Rob asked, "Are you all right?" sounding concerned.

"No, I'm not," I murmured.

Without hesitation, Rob replied, "Hold on." He broke off rounds and arranged for the team to continue rounding with another resident.

Alone, I stepped into a short hallway off the main corridor, near a window. Examining my silhouette in the glass, I tried to stay strong even at my lowest. As I waited for Rob to join me, I stared blankly out of the window from the sixteenth floor. The rusted locks on the windows prevented me from acting on my impulse to free myself from my suffocating shame.

I could jump out of this window, and it would all be over. I wiped the tears from my eyes and tried to man up, dreading having to spill my emotions and show weakness to a white guy I barely knew. But I had to face the music. My options were few.

"So what's going on?" Rob asked.

"I feel like I'm out of control. I'm just going through the motions. I don't know what's going on with my patients, and I feel like I might make a mistake or something," I responded honestly.

In truth, I felt like I might have accidentally killed someone. The more I spoke, the more my tears fell. And all the while I could not take my mind off that window just two feet away.

"Let's talk to Holly," Rob replied.

I nodded my head in the agreement.

Holly was the chief medical resident in charge of the interns and residents. She had finished the training program four years earlier and also completed a cardiology fellowship. She was smart, pretty, accomplished, down to earth, and liked by everyone, it seemed. Holly was a golden girl with a heart of gold. We sat in her office, and she sorted the whole thing out within twenty minutes.

"Look, LaMar, we have every confidence in your abilities. We chose you on our first rank-list because we were really impressed with you. I have no doubt that you can be a star in this program. It sounds like since you've been here, there have been a lot of things going on in your personal life," Holly said.

I agreed, slowly nodding.

"Why don't you take a week off to get your life in order? After you get settled, we'll start you back on the step-down unit for two weeks."

"Step-down?" What was that? Was I about to be demoted? I had no idea what Holly was talking about.

"Yes. This service is much slower than the medical wards. You work together with the resident, finish by six o'clock every day, and there's no call. This way we can ease you back in over two weeks before going back to the wards," she said.

Having never seen or heard of this service, I couldn't imagine what she was describing. To be honest, it kind of sounded like a remedial rotation to me. But I was in no real position to negotiate terms.

"Okay. I think that'll work," I responded. I sighed happily, knowing that I would live to fight for my dream at least one more day.

I was thankful that Holly expressed confidence in me. When I left her office, I felt relieved but no less burdened. I walked through the hallway and down four flights of stairs. Pushing open the glass doors, I stepped outside of the hospital onto Sixty-Eighth Street and into the sun. I took a long, deep breath of my new beginning, finally able to decompress.

For the first couple of days of my respite, I walked around the city contemplating my fate, often riding the subway with no particular destination. I looked blankly into the faces of strangers. Did they have fates that were so uncertain? Were they on life's bubble like me?

The bustling streets of Upper Eastside Manhattan were big enough to swallow me and my problems whole. I needed only to surrender. Large trucks and crowded buses blew past me, and I thought, *Just two side steps into traffic, LaMar. Two steps, and it's all over.*

PART 1
G STREET

1 | Layout

NEIGHBORHOOD

Many years ago, I read somewhere that the ghetto is not a physical location. It's a state of mind. If this is true, I can argue with confidence that I did not grow up in the ghetto. The little house, all 462 square feet of it, located at 4497 G Street was not located in the ghetto. And the residents on that street were not ghettoized.

From birth to age twelve, my entire world was geographically bound by two public elementary schools, a small welfare office, the Food-o-Rama grocery store that stocked bad meat, and Sally's candy store. With the exception of regular trips to my grandparents' house and my annual summer pilgrimage to Pasadena, my universe was no bigger than about five square miles.

G Street was a plush place to grow up in the seventies. The fact that most of the families were sustained on welfare didn't matter much. A happy child doesn't realize his station in life until he becomes old enough to make comparisons himself or experience the sting of prejudice for being poor or different.

On G Street, there were black families, Mexican families, Samoans, and a few elderly white couples that probably couldn't afford to leave, even as the neighborhood changed all around them. The neighborhood also had Christians, Catholics, Muslims, and nonbelievers. Families got to know one another, the children played together, and young people respected their elders.

The thing that made that place so glorious for me was that there were so many kids, and we all played together. G Street was the playground for nearly a hundred kids of every age, shape, and color. I learned to keep myself entertained during long summer days. Like most kids on G Street, I improvised, making up games and rules as the day went along.

Tree climbing, roof jumping, and a game we called smear the queer, which I can only describe as ghetto rugby, weren't exactly conventional sports, but they were common athletic competitions in my neighborhood. There was nothing negative about the word *queer* the way we used it to describe the game. It was a full-contact sport that could be played with nothing more than an object. We used a ball, shoe, Frisbee, or even a rolled-up shirt or sock worked well. Similar to rugby, the objective of the game was simply to pick up the item, whatever it was, and try to run for daylight. Much like a fumbled football, any person picking up the object would get jumped, or smeared, with no thought about getting hurt.

In my world of made-up games, a conventional game, kickball, was the official sport of the neighborhood. It appealed to everyone. Maybe because the game was so simple, the rules were never contested, and anyone could play regardless of his or her size or athletic ability. A small kid like me would be picked for a team just as often as a big kid, as long as he or she had a big foot. Kick the ball and run to the base. That I could do like the rest of them.

"I got LaMar," one of the team captains would call out as the teams were chosen.

"I got Billy!" "I got Andre!" "I got Lynn!" "I got Paula!" The captains went back and forth until every kid that wanted to play was picked for one team or the other.

We played in the middle of the street. A flattened milk carton or tin can served as home plate and second base. First and third bases were usually the door handle on a parked car and the telephone pole on opposite sides of the street. Although I excelled at many games, I was best at dares that required athletic ability, like jumping from rooftops at the nearby elementary schools into the sandbox down below, climbing the highest branches of the great tree that sat in my front yard, or scaling up the bungalows at Chollas Elementary School and then running and jumping from rooftop to rooftop, spanning a distance of five feet, twelve feet above the hot, broken asphalt below.

At the age of ten, without batting an eyelash, I tested my speed, agility, and nerve on the ultimate proving ground—the interstate highway.

It was hotter than July. Billy and I had begun our long walk home from the hardware store located on Federal Boulevard and Forty-Seventh Street. It was more than an hour by foot, but I had a better idea.

"Where are you going?" Billy asked.

"Just follow me!" I shouted.

Running ahead, I figured that if we jumped the fence alongside the Coca-Cola bottling plant, slid down the dirt embankment, and sprinted across I-94, we could cut through Holy Cross Cemetery and shave off thirty minutes from our long walk home.

I dared Billy, who was thirteen at the time, to race me across the freeway.

"I double dare you to race me," I said to Billy.

"Race … where?" Billy looked across the eight-lane span of highway and back at me, his eyes bucked, his head shaking an adamant no. "You're crazy!"

Maybe I was crazy. The challenge excited me.

"On the count of three," I said fearlessly. After counting down, I took off, crossing four westbound lanes of the highway to the halfway point, and ended up straddling the center divider. Billy stood trembling on the embankment. Stuck out there alone, I couldn't believe my fate. Maybe I wasn't so crazy after all. My heart beat out of control.

As I waited there for Billy, cars whisked by at sixty-five miles per hour, nearly blowing me over. People honked their horns and yelled out of their car windows at me. They were moving too fast for me to understand what they were saying, but instinctively I knew. The longer I sat out there clutching the median, the more distressed I became. After nearly ten minutes of clinging to the center railing, I decided to sprint back to join Billy, who had been frantically waving me back the whole time.

It was common for me to take big risks. For example, the times I hopped the fence at the Jackie Robinson YMCA to go swimming afterhours. During the regular hours of operation, I had to pay a quarter, fuss with the lifeguards, and put up with bumping heads with every other kid within a twenty-mile radius. Besides, I wasn't allowed to wear cutoffs. The swimsuit requirement was a huge inconvenience because swim trunks were not standard gear for me. My shorts were made from the previous year's pants that I outgrew. It was far better for me to do my own thing. So I would easily climb the nine-foot chain-link fence, strip down to my underwear, and have a cool swim by myself. I wasn't a strong swimmer, but I could dog paddle all day. The prospect of drowning never occurred to me. In my mind, I was invincible.

DEVINE ECHOES
Bam, bam, bam!

That loud banging on my front door came like clockwork. For an old lady, Mrs. Roberts had a loud knock. My spiritual mother, Mrs. Mae Francis Roberts, was my guide to God. She was my grandmother's age and lived on G Street right next-door to us.

Dang! Is it that time again? It was. Tuesdays always seemed to creep up on me. Tuesday afternoons meant one thing: it was time to go clean the church. The angel on my right shoulder reminded me that it was the Lord's work, as Mrs. Roberts called it. The devil on my left shoulder tried to convince me that my time was better spent shooting marbles with friends or watching the idiot box.

Mom called out, "LaMar, you ready to go?"

With my mother's prompting, the angel in me always won out. I dreaded going, especially since my siblings and the other kids on G Street always flaked out. I hated that Mrs. Roberts saw me as little Mr. Reliable.

Mrs. Roberts drove below the speed limit, ensuring that our trip would take longer than it needed to take. With the gospel channel on a low volume, she'd chat me up, asking questions about my schoolwork or my friends. I would answer politely and with all the honesty that I thought she could handle, shifting my body constantly to adjust to the worn vinyl seats that pricked the underside of my legs.

That concentrated time alone with an adult that cared about me made me feel special, like the Lord's child. She would drive, and when I wasn't shifting in my seat or struggling to peer over the dashboard, I would sometimes study her plump, rough hands wrapped around the steering wheel, and her dark complexion. Her salt and pepper hair was short, pressed straight, and greased back. Her glasses sat halfway down the bridge of her nose just above her fixed smile. Short and round, Mrs. Roberts was made from the kind of black that didn't crack. She was old, but her skin never revealed just how old she was. For all of the years that I knew her, she never seemed to age. Not one single year.

The Church of God was located down on the corner of Franklin and Clay Streets, in the part of San Diego called Logan Heights. A small, one-story, white brick stucco building that sat on a small lot, it had barely eighty members in attendance on any given Sunday. When it was full, like on Easter Sunday, it could hold nearly three hundred. I knew that church better than most members because I cleaned it. No sooner would we pull up to the curve than we'd spring into action. Mrs. Roberts was driven to work unto the Lord, but I was just trying to get it done and over with so that I could get back home in time enough to watch *Happy Days*, *Laverne and Shirley*, or *Good Times*, whatever I could catch before bedtime.

Each week, I dreaded having to volunteer to clean the church, but once on the job, all rebellion left my spirit. A two-person cleaning brigade, Mrs. Roberts took care of the ladies' room and kitchen areas. I ran the vacuum up and down the narrow aisles of the sanctuary, putting worn fans with pictures of Martin Luther King Jr., Ms. Mahalia Jackson, and the Greenwood Mortuary on them into the slots behind the pews where they were kept for service. The faces pictured on the fans were black, but the faces on the walls were not. A white, blonde-haired, blue-eyed Jesus nailed to the cross was located above the pulpit. To the left of the pulpit was a wooden board that was supposed to keep track of the weekly tithes collected, but it never changed. On the opposite wall hung a large framed picture of the Prince of Peace wearing a crown of thorns, his face pained, strained toward the heavens as blood dripped down his golden locks and a tear slid from one eye.

Sometimes while rolling up the vacuum cord or straightening out the small bottles of olive oil near the altar, I'd search for the meaning of life in the dated brush strokes of white Jesus on that faded painting.

"God, Jesus, are you here? Well then say something." At nine years old, I dared the picture to talk to me.

Alone in the empty sanctuary, I swallowed hard while I tested the Holy Spirit. I halfway hoped to see a tear dripping down the canvas or some bright glow illuminating the face of white Jesus. But the better part of me hoped for no such signs. After collecting candy and gum wrappers, lightly dusting, and fluffing worn-out seat cushions, I left the sanctuary and made my way to the men's bathroom where I cleaned the toilet and sink and polished the mirror. By the time I finished, Mrs. Roberts had come around to check my work.

"Praise God. Praise God," she'd say, nodding with a big smile as she inspected my work.

Gushing with pride, I received my big squeeze and "God bless you" from Mrs. Roberts, which I hoped might save me the next time I stepped out of line. God knows that I was lucky to have never been struck by lightning for the devilish things I did outside of the church.

Although my mother rarely attended church, she made sure her kids were there every Sunday wearing our best clothes, starched and pressed. Between me, my brothers and sister, and Mrs. Robert's children, who were older, her baby-blue station wagon was packed every Sunday. Looking out the back window as we pulled away, I thought about all the fun I would miss out on, watching cartoons and running through the streets with friends like Carla and Lynn and Billy.

Every now and again, Mrs. Roberts convinced Billy's mother to send him to church with us. I wondered if Mrs. Roberts ever regretted bringing him. Billy was a source of high entertainment during church. I looked forward to his rare attendance. Small in stature with a short Afro that looked more like a tight-knit skullcap, Billy looked like a young Flip Wilson, a comedian with a weekly variety show at the time. The kids on G Street feared Billy not for his might but for his tongue. His sharp wit allowed him to fire jokes about you or your mama nonstop until he embarrassed you to silence.

"Your mama is so black she sweats coffee." Billy had jokes for days. But he was his funniest when he went to church. Whenever the sanctuary prayed on bended knee, Billy was in rare comedic form.

"Yes, Lawd."

"Yes, Jesus!"

"Thank ya, Jesus!

"Hallelujah!"

"Yes, brother, yes!"

Billy's voice was heard above all the others in the congregation. His eyes were wide open. He'd nudge me and my brother LaSalle in his mockery. It was a riot. My eyes watered so much it looked like I was overcome with emotion. They were tears of joy that I could barely contain. The fact that he couldn't be punished made his performances even more outrageous. No one could caution him because, for all they knew, he was praying to God. You know, touched by the spirit. I knew better.

When the prayer ended, Billy let out the loudest "Amen, Lord. A-a-a-men!" He said it so convincingly you'd thought he was the deacon called to lead the prayer. Then he'd get up off his knees and with a straight face grab his seat alongside my brother and me. Older members of the church shot disapproving glares at Billy, but he didn't care. I loved those rare Sundays when Billy came to church. It seemed to make the mornings fly.

"You coming next week?" I'd ask Billy when church ended.

"Yeah. We'll see." He'd always answer the same, but I knew that meant I wouldn't see him back in church for months.

When Mrs. Roberts wasn't around, and the Prince of Peace portrait wasn't hovering over my head, I wasn't always little Mr. Reliable. Cleverly, I figured out a way keep my church offering. The trick was easy. I dropped my dollar into the collection plate and removed four quarters, appearing as though I was getting change. With my heart pounding, fingers sweating, and eyes sheepishly downcast, I made a clean swap. My soul belonged to God, but my stomach and my dollar were pledged to Dolly Madison. I had just enough time to walk to the store during the break between services and buy an apple pie or Ding Dong cupcakes. So it came as a surprise to me when I arrived to take my regular seat on the right-hand side of Mrs. Roberts one Sunday morning and looked down to find a masking tape label placed on a brand-new seat cushion that read, "Little Brother LaMar." There were new pillows for all the saints and elders, but I was the only kid in the entire church to have my very own.

Long-time churchgoers in good standing were always referred to as "brother" or "sister" or "mother" so and so. Mrs. Roberts, for example, went by the name Sister Roberts or Sister Mae Francis. It seemed that I had graduated to "little brother" status. Finally, all of the time I spent cleaning toilets during the week, vacuuming the sanctuary, and collecting tin cans for the church van fund had paid off. Or maybe God had forgiven my transgressions. Sure, the church was filled with a bunch of fakes, people who acted one way in the sanctuary and lived a completely different life once out in the real world. Sometimes people would curse you out in the parking lot leaving church. But Mrs. Roberts was the real deal. I sat on the right-hand side of a true saint for years. I watched her flip through her tattered, large-print, red-letter-edition Bible, searching for scriptures with her glasses perched halfway down her nose. I knelt down beside her for prayer on countless Sundays, she with her thick knee-highs rolled just beneath her plump knees, and me in my church clothes. Fortunately, some of her Christian ways rubbed off on me.

The Church of God was small, and the Sunday sermons were simple, but it was where I learned life's basic tenets of morality. It was there that I learned about humility, sacrifice, honesty and how to treat people right and settle disputes nonviolently. The good book lists "Thou shalt not kill" as one of the Ten Commandments. Therefore, taking one's own life was forbidden. That I knew, even if I hadn't learned anything else.

2 | Miles Apart

It was Christmas Eve 1973, and tucked under our small white plastic Christmas tree was a special gift for me from my dad, Levi "Lee" Hasbrouck. Just days before, he made a rare visit to drop off presents.

"You got it, son?" Lee asked me.

Struggling to help him unload a heap of wrapped presents, I had my eyes on one particular box with my name on it.

"Yeah, I got it!" I said excitedly as I followed him into the house.

"All right then, son. You listen to your mother," Lee said, with a timid glance toward my mom. After barely setting the gifts on the floor, Lee left our house and vanished into thin air before the screen door closed behind him. I called my father by his first name. His absence from my life never made me comfortable enough to call him dad. It never felt right, and he never corrected me.

When Christmas morning arrived, I tore through the wrapping paper to discover a football helmet and shoulder pads. For the next few weeks, I purposely unleashed a personal assault against every wall and fence post that I could find, banging my body around with reckless abandon. Lee's gift ignited my love affair with contact sports, and football in particular. As it turned out, that one extraordinary gift would be the largest contribution he would make to my life.

Most memories of Christmas with my father were very different. Lee lived in Pasadena, California, which was a three-hour train ride from San Diego. Every summer for a span of about six years,

I'd visit him for a week at a time. Occasionally I would visit him during Christmas. Christmas in Pasadena always sparkled. It was not mine to savor, but I could experience it secondhand through my younger brother, Rafael. Conceived from my father's second marriage to a white woman, Rafael made out like a bandit every Christmas. Unfortunately, being an only child, he never learned how to share the wealth. He had plenty of things sitting under a large, fresh-cut Fraser fir tree that scraped the ceiling. He would open one gift after another before my bulging eyes. All I could do was watch with eager anticipation as he unveiled his latest new toy, game, or gizmo. *They aren't my toys*, I thought, *but maybe I can play with a few of them when he's not looking or after he goes to sleep.*

Looking back on it now, it was a pretty cruel joke my father played, dragging his abandoned kids to Pasadena for one week out of the entire year only to expose us to a new wife who sweetly tolerated us and a half brother who was spoiled rotten. But it never occurred to me to begrudge my little brother anything. Plain and simple, I saw him as better than me. More loved. Even as a little boy, I reasoned that Rafael had to be better because he had better pajamas, better toys, and a better house. He grew up with cabinets stocked with food and two dogs to play with. I didn't have any of that. He had a mother and *my* father to boot. It stood to reason that his Christmases would be better than mine.

Without the painful reminder of the lopsided gift giving, things seemed more evenhanded during summer visits. Sometimes Lee planned a trip to Universal Studios or Disneyland. Sometimes it was a fishing trip or local family gathering. No matter what he planned, it was the highlight of my summer. It was far better than hanging around on G Street, attending summer school, or eating bologna and butter sandwiches from the Neighborhood House Association, a community-based charity.

During my most memorable summer visit, I went on a weekend truck drive with Lee. Everyone was clamoring to go, but I drew the long straw. It was the longest stretch of concentrated time that I ever had alone with my biological father. Sitting in silence next to a man

14

that I barely knew, I fantasized that it was one of many interstate road trips we'd taken together.

Lee was a tall, slender, rugged-appearing man with a wiry mustache that bent down slightly at the corners of his mouth. He wore a short Afro and usually had a cigarette hanging off his bottom lip and a can of beer in his hand. A man's man, Lee fished, worked with his hands, and drove an 18-wheeler. Quiet but approachable, Lee always seemed to be working around his three-bedroom house, fixing something. As we sat side by side, I examined him. He sat strong in the saddle of his monster truck, wearing a T-shirt, with one sleeve turned up to hold his cigarettes. His worn trousers, dusty boots, and confident grip on the steering wheel told the story of a road-tested veteran.

"How are you doing, son?" he'd ask from time to time.

Watching the miles pass in my side-view mirror, almost hypnotized by the mile markers racing by, I snapped to attention. "I'm okay."

"We'll stop to get something to eat in a little while," he said.

"Okay," I replied politely, contemplating if this man would someday grow to be my hero.

Lee never asked me about my progress in school or my friends. He didn't ask about life on G Street or my wishes or dreams. There I sat, his ten-year-old son, and he said next to nothing to me. *Why did you leave Mom? Why don't you ever call on my birthday? Why does Rafael get everything and I get nothing?* There were lots of questions swirling around in my head, and I was burning to ask them all, but I didn't dare. From my point of view, Lee had some explaining to do, and our road trip seemed like the perfect time for him to come clean. Was it my responsibility to ask the obvious questions? If only I had the courage. Instead, I sat paralyzed. Lee ignored the awkward silence, pressed the gas pedal, and left my questions and curiosities in his rearview mirror like so many oil-slicked miles of interstate.

If bonding were to happen between father and son, it would not take place during that adventure. The sad fact of the matter was that my father and I were strangers. Despite me longing for a connection, he never made any efforts to be a father. Sadly, he divorced me along with my mother. I never felt malice toward Lee. What I felt, if not indifferent, was a gaping void of emotion for him. The memories of the train rides to Pasadena on the Amtrak shine brighter than the actual time spent with my biological dad and his replacement family. It was probably the sense of adventure or excitement that comes with being someplace fresh, other than G Street, that accounted for my bliss. Unfortunately, those trips dried up as the years went on. By the time I was twelve, they had stopped completely. Outside of sending for us during the summers, my football gear, and an occasional Christmas visit, Lee sent twenty-five dollars for child support for about three months and then stopped. He was a deadbeat dad who never looked back. Over the years, I invited him to every major milestone in my life, but he never bothered to show up or even acknowledge the occasion with a card or phone call. Maybe that's why I ignored him emotionally, reducing him in my mind to a nonfactor throughout the years.

My father left my mother when I was about eighteen months old. He had been slipping out to Pasadena more and more to spend time with his girlfriend. When my mother confronted him, he became violent. That was the straw that broke the camel's back. My mother had taken enough beatings as a kid, and she wasn't about to take a beating as a grown woman. She matched him blow for blow during one final clash and then cut her losses. She told him that he could go back to Pasadena to be with his girlfriend and stay there. That's what he did. On his way out, Lee bitterly swore to my mother that no one would ever want a single woman with three kids. As it turned out, he couldn't have been more wrong.

SMITTY'S RUN

My mother was taking night classes at Lincoln High School to earn her general education diploma, or GED, when she met James E. Smith. Smitty, as his boys called him, was also working on his GED. Arrested by my mother's bright smile and pretty brown eyes, Smitty struck up a conversation and eventually got up the nerve to ask her out. He was so smitten with my mother that he would rather spend nights in his car, down at the end of G Street, than go a day without her company. My grandmother, Mimi, eventually took pity on him and allowed him to move in with us. Smitty became my first in-house father of memory because I never had any recollection of Lee living in our home.

Mom and Smitty were never married. But during the six or so years that Smitty lived with us, I had the makings of a traditional family. There were regular family dinners and occasional family outings. Like the 1974 movie *Claudine*, starring Diahann Carroll and James Earl Jones, my childhood was rich with love but poor materially.

"Hey, baby, I'm stepping out for a minute," Smitty would say to my mother, almost out of the clear blue, it seemed.

"Where are you going?" Mom asked, no doubt sensing some foolishness.

"I'll be right back," Smitty fired back before he blew out the door. My mom's words chased behind him but rarely hooked him. Smitty seldom turned back. He was accustomed to doing his own thing, coming and going as he pleased. My mom, on the other hand, was expected to stay close to home.

"Bastard!" my mom shouted.

The scenario was unpredictably predictable and replayed like a broken record. The word bastard was shouted so many times that I wanted to know what it meant. So one day I asked.

"Mom, what's a bastard?"

"That's none of your business, boy. Now sit yourself down somewhere before I whup your behind. And don't ever let me catch you saying that word again, you hear?" my mom answered.

Perplexed, I responded, "Yes, Mama." Then I went somewhere to sit my butt down as instructed. She didn't help clarify things at all. But I knew better than to push it.

Smitty was a chocolate-brown, clean-shaven, cool breeze of a brother. He had a lean, athletic build and a big Afro. He was also a ladies' man not quite ready for monogamous family life. He boosted his legitimate income by shooting dice every weekend in back rooms at house parties that took place when the clubs let out. He was good at it too, pulling down a few hundred dollars every weekend. It was a dangerous way to make a few extra dollars. That's why Smitty packed a gun, just in case things got rowdy. He made money fast and spent it even faster. Always the sharp dresser, Smitty did his part to keep up his hustler image, making regular trips to the Los Angeles garment district for fabric and tailor-made suits.

When Smitty was not at home, he enjoyed hanging out with his boys Big Red and Forney. He never brought other women around the house, but judging from my mom's response, that didn't prevent them from occasionally calling the house. When my mom intercepted a call or discovered lipstick on Smitty's collar, a big argument erupted. A few days would pass before they would make up, and only then could I breathe a sigh of relief, thankful that my family remained intact. Eventually, my mom grew tired of his double-standard shenanigans and sent him packing. His fate was like the rare box of sugarcoated name-brand cereal in our home: one day there for everyone to enjoy, the next day gone without a trace. Smitty just up and disappeared. One morning I awoke, and he was gone.

Smitty was my first in-house father after Lee left. When Smitty and my mother split up, my siblings and I began to refer to him as Marvin's father, or James. As I grew into manhood, I would affectionately come to call him Smitty, or simply Pops. He earned that distinction because, unlike Lee, Smitty stayed connected. At every graduation, birthday, wedding, funeral, and major family event, Smitty was there, and he remains in my life to this very day. If fatherhood were a relay race, I would credit Smitty with running a respectable leg—fast out of the blocks, stumbling a bit, then running out of steam. His six-year leg was fantastic compared to my biological father, Lee, who barely got out of the starting blocks before throwing in the towel and starting from scratch with another woman. But just like Lee, Smitty dropped the baton short of the finish line.

SQUARE ONE

Single again, my mother moved on. Apparently there were plenty of eligible bachelors that didn't mind dating a single woman with four kids, especially one as pretty as her. A licensed cosmetologist and part-time model, her attention to beauty showed in everything she did. With her caramel-colored skin, big brown eyes, killer figure, and a full complement of wigs, she could pass for Diana Ross on a bad day. She even held the official title as one of the Ten Best-Dressed Women in San Diego.

My grandparents lived less than fifteen minutes away, so it was easy for Mom to drop her kids off and have child-free weekends. It was no picnic staying at my grandparents' house. My grandmother, Mimi, was slight in stature but could wield a switch, her weapon of choice for corporal punishment, with stinging accuracy. My grandfather, Poppa, was a former chief petty officer in the US Navy. He was short, fat, bald, and cantankerous, and he ran his house like a ship deck, constantly barking out orders. His stern eyes tracked us everywhere we went. He was quick to lay the leather strap to our behinds when we stepped out of line. Poppa was so dominant that he determined what we ate, when we ate, if we could butter our bread and use condiments on our food, and when we could drink our glass of milk with our meal.

"Boy, put that glass down! I don't want you drinking anything until after you've eaten everything on that plate," Poppa demanded. His heavy meals sat stubbornly in the back of my throat, nearly choking me to death. I did my best to produce enough saliva to force each bite down my esophagus without a cold glass of milk or water. I never felt welcomed at my grandparents' house as a child. Not really. To be in Poppa's navy felt almost like a punishment, to tell the truth. My sister, Jaeneen, received VIP treatment as my grandmother's favorite.

"Where's my Suga'?" Mimi would carry on about Jaeneen as she whisked past my brothers and me, looking for her. Invisible until my bad behavior required correcting, I was just one of three nappy-headed boys prone to mischief.

"Bell, you need to cut that ol' sheep's wool off that boy's head," she'd say. She called my mom Bell and never Beverly, her actual name.

Every time Mimi suggested a haircut, I cringed because I cherished my hair. An Afro defined a young blood back in the mid-1970s. The bigger Afro you wore, rounded and parted on the side, the cooler you were. It was my lion's mane. It didn't matter that I couldn't see the back of my head, which was usually a matted bed-headed mess. I loved the parts I could see.

My grandparents were judgmental, overly critical, and firm; they shared traits common among most grandparents, I guess. But behind it all, there was the kind of love that moved them to keep us nearly every other weekend. Unfortunately, too often tensions would rise between my mother and Poppa, and we'd get caught in the crosshairs. One night when my mother came to pick the four of us up from my grandparents' house, she got into a shouting match with Poppa.

"You're right. These are my kids. I will make sure that they eat. C'mon, kids. Get your things. Let's go," my mother demanded.

The entire argument took place in the entrance of the front door. Mom barely stepped into my grandparents' house. It sounded like the argument was about them not feeding us and my mother coming to pick us up late. Whatever the case, it was enough to piss my mother off. We ate at Jack in the Box that night. We ordered drive-through and finished our food during the short, tense, silent ride home.

Emotionally drained, my mother sent us to bed the minute we got home, and then she cried herself to sleep. Feeling her pain without even quite understanding it, I did the same. That night, like so many other nights before that, was a painful reminder of just how powerless I was over my circumstances. With no father to care for me, and a mother struggling to make ends meet, I sat in bed thinking about just how small my world was and just how tiny, almost insignificant, I was within it.

3 | Brave

The little house that I grew up in had one bathroom and two bedrooms. One room was small, and the other was tiny. The tiniest room accommodated me, my two brothers, and my sister. My mother squeezed in two sets of bunk beds. The sets were so close together that I could hold hands with my bunkmate on the other set. Being third oldest, I was assigned to a top bunk, above my sister.

My sister, Jaeneen, was the oldest. My grandmother, Mimi, called her Suga' and spoiled her sweet. Growing up, my sister was second in charge. My mother empowered her to boss my brothers and me around in her absence. She cooked, cleaned like the rest of us, and kept a watchful eye on her boys. She could not beat us, but she could, and would, tell my mother on us, which had the same effect. Jaeneen took her responsibilities seriously. That was never more evident than the time she went toe to toe with the neighborhood bully on my behalf. Crying, I ran home to tell my sister that he was picking on me.

"Where is he now?" she asked.

I pushed open the screen door and pointed down the street. Without a moment of hesitation, Jaeneen marched down the street with my brothers and me in tow to confront the boy. And like all good neighborhood squabbles about to go down, we picked up kids along the way. By the time we arrived at our destination, there was a crowd of curious kids numbering more than a dozen.

It was a dusk summer night. We all stood in the middle of the street waiting for the first spark to light up the showdown at the O.K. Corral. Then it happened. In what must have taken an act of maternal bravery, Jaeneen confronted the older boy to his face.

"I heard you were messing with my brother," she stated.

"So what," he replied blatantly. Pooky was a chubby boy who liked to throw his weight around. He was two years older than my sister and outweighed her by at least twenty-five pounds. But that didn't stop her from giving him a stern warning to stop messing with her boys—or else.

In defiance, Pooky fired back, "You're not about to do nothing!"

Then he did something that I am sure he regrets to this day.

"Here, punch me right here if you got the nerve. I dare you." He stuck his face out, closed his eyes, and dared my sister to take a swing by pointing to his nose. My sister didn't flinch. Like greased lightning, she hauled back and broke that boy's nose against her knuckles. His knees buckled, and he fell on his behind.

"That was nothing. I bet she wouldn't try that again," he said as he wiped his bleeding nose and tried to regain his composure.

My sister stood silent but ready. Pooky stood to his feet, but he never made a move to retaliate. The standoff was over. I turned and walked with my big sister triumphantly back to our house and never looked back. She didn't either. She may have been filled with fear, but I couldn't tell it by looking at her. The word of my sister's knockout spread through the neighborhood like wildfire. As a result of her rep, I had another layer of protection.

My brother LaSalle, who is one year older than me, had the bunk directly across from me. Whereas I resembled nothing of the man listed on my birth certificate, LaSalle embodied him. He took on Lee's looks, deep voice, mannerisms, his talent for building and fixing things, and many of his other characteristics. I, on the other hand, borrowed heavily from my mother's physical features, her creativity, her sense of exploration, and her ability to plan and be patient.

LaSalle seemed to miss Lee the most. I guess longing for a father is what made him more vulnerable to certain snares in the neighborhood, which led him down the harder path. Still, as a big brother growing up, LaSalle was there for me. My selection for the school safety patrol was because of him. It came with the responsibility of guiding kids across a busy Market Street. That responsibility gave me status. I wore a cardinal-red cardigan, white pants, a white dress shirt, a black belt, and a red soldier boy cover. That was the official uniform. Because of LaSalle, I received promotions faster than the other safety guards, going from the rank of private to staff sergeant in a matter of weeks, not months. LaSalle also taught me how to patch flat tires, do minor bike repairs, and make stilts and go-carts from the surplus scrap wood that we took from the construction site during the expansion of the Interstate 805. And, of course, when I needed coaching about girls, it was big brother's advice that guided me. It's fair to say that LaSalle taught me all that my father didn't.

The last edition to Mom's brood was Marvin. He arrived on the scene not long after Smitty moved in. Come to think of it, that may have been the reason why Mimi let him move into the house. He eventually slept in the bottom bunk bed, just across from Jaeneen. With an easy smile and big puffy Afro, Marvin Akili "Fatso" Smith was a happy kid brother from the beginning. He was more chocolate than the rest of us because he took the complexion of Smitty. Marvin was a precocious kid with a gift for gab and talent for learning dances. He never saw a dance that he could not replicate. I would sometimes break down under the harsh criticism of my family whenever I tried to learn a new dance move, despite practicing for hours. Marvin, on the other hand, could master any dance he saw in about five minutes. Marvin was never considered my half brother. Despite having a different biological father than me, he was, and remains to this day, purely my brother.

The two sets of bunk beds allowed me and my siblings to share our day's adventures at bedtime. Some nights the four of us would stay up for hours talking. Whether as a caretaker, a builder, a daredevil, or an entertainer, my siblings and I learned how to be brave. We were individuals, each with our unique personalities, talents, and interests, but we grew up close in part because of our sardine-like rooming arrangements. Little did I know, those tight quarters—and, in fact, my whole world—was about to expand.

4 | Mama's Hand

My sister may have had the part-time duty of keeping me and her other boys in check during the after-school hours, but the full-time assignment fell on my mother. With no consistent father around to keep track of my whereabouts, I would've run wild if not for the stern hand of my mother. Moms may have occasionally spoiled the child, but she never spared the rod, a biblical principle I came to learn all too well. Some parents in the hood used those bright orange plastic racetracks from the Hot Wheels racecar sets to spank their kids. Other parents used whatever they could get their hands on in the heat of the moment. The most dreaded thing to get beat with, bar none, was the extension cord. It was medieval. The cord cut into your flesh like nothing else. Some kids in my neighborhood got the cord on a regular basis. Their skin, especially their arms and legs, was scarred with defensive wounds mirroring the stages of healing. To be on the receiving end of the cord in my house meant that you did something incomprehensible. Thank God I never caught the cord, but a few times I came dangerously close.

Like most kids on the block, we were made to follow a short list of universal rules. These included no company in the house when my mother was gone, no talking back, having the house cleaned by the time my mother got home for work, and being inside the house before the streetlights went on. There were rare exceptions when I was allowed to play in the streets at night, like when Moms had a Tupperware party or some other grown folks' social event at the house. But my friends were never allowed in the house when my mom was not home—period. No exceptions. For some reason, sneaking friends in the house always seemed worth risking a butt beating.

Before my mom saved up enough money for a reliable car, she traveled back and forth to work compliments of the San Diego Transit Authority. Her Buick Electra 225, or deuce and a quarter, rarely worked. It was more like a huge lawn ornament than viable transportation. The car rested on the dirt lot in front of our house. We played in, on top of, and around it. Our only warning of her arrival was the screeching sound of the brakes from the public bus.

"Mom's coming!" my sister would shout, peeking out of the window after hearing the screeching sounds of the bus brakes, the sighing sound of air pistons forcing the doors open, and the revving of the engine. The bus stopped every hour, on the hour. Like roaches scattering when the kitchen light is flicked on in the middle of the night, we scrambled, tripping over one another, opening and closing doors to let our company out of the house. We did everything humanly possible to comply with Mom's house rules after the fact, with little time to spare.

The bus stop was a stone's throw away from our house, at the corner of Market Street and Forty-Fifth Street. The distance was too short to put all our friends out and clean up the entire house before Moms dragged in from the corner. We heard keys rattle right before the door flew open. My mom was quick to notice that the house wasn't clean.

"After you finish cleaning up this house, I want somebody to get me my belt!" she would announce.

The rod in our house was usually a leather belt. We called our beatings whippings. And just about every day it seemed like my mother was laying the leather to someone's backside. It was uncommon for one of us to get a whipping without the other three standing in line for theirs as well. We were collectively responsible for having the house clean. Since the house was the size of a cracker box, the chores were not extensive. But everyone was expected to pitch in. I learned how to make up my bed properly by about the time I stopped wetting it, how to wash, dry, and put dishes away by age seven, and how to clean the base of the toilet with a Pine-Sol soaked sponge by age eight. When we had to be, we were human vacuum cleaners, picking up lint and debris from the floor on our hands and knees. Unfortunately, many nights we'd fall short of her expectations. When my mother promised us a whipping, we followed protocol. The first thing we did was the roll call.

"I'm first," one of us said.

"I'm last," the next person chimed in.

"Second."

"All right, I'll go third."

And with that, the order that we lined up at the arm of the couch was set. There were no deviations, no power plays at the last minute. There was no seniority. If you called a place in the order, you got it.

There was a sound rationale for the order. Going first meant that you got it over with first. You were the first to dry your tears and clear the stuttering hiccups that came from crying uncontrollably. Being first was the best place in the order. If you couldn't call first, you called last. Here you were playing the odds that Mom got tired by the time she was four deep into the butt-whipping rotation. If you were lucky, she might run out of steam, in which case the duration of your whipping was short-lived. Or she might just break down into tears. That happened sometimes but not too often. If it did, you could avoid a whipping altogether. For that reason, being last was the next best place in the lineup. The second and third slots were essentially neutral positions. You were somewhere in the middle of the order. You had no advantages.

When the time of reckoning came, after all the chores were done, Mom called for us. We lined up in our set order and began our sad, slow march to the arm of the couch.

"Who's first?" she'd ask.

Then one by one we would peel down our clothes and bend over the padded arm of the couch, jackknife fashion, with our face buried in the cushions and our bare butts pointed toward the sky. If I cried loud enough, she sometimes took mercy on me. If I overdid the crying, she whipped me harder and longer for carrying on with all the added drama. My hands flew back instinctively to cover my blistering behind. It was unavoidable. But too much blocking frustrated her too.

"Move your hands! Boy, I said move your hands!" Mom yelled, striking a mighty blow with each word she uttered. "If you don't move those hands, you're gonna get more!"

One night I guessed wrong during roll call. I called first when I should have called last. My mother snapped and went ballistic on me. My brothers and sister looked on with paralyzed horror as my mother took out all of her frustration on me and only me. That night was about more than undone chores. With each blow, I felt the gut-wrenching pain of a single mother with sore feet and swollen ankles from standing all day trying to squeak out a living and struggling to raise four children. She desperately wanted to shed the indignity of needing welfare and every heartbreaking disappointment along the way. That night I absorbed the wrath of a young life filled with regret.

"I don't know why you kids won't listen! I am so tired of beating your butts I don't know what to do!" Her rage ended when she threw the belt against the wall and collapsed to the floor crying, holding her face in her hands, her back against her bed.

"We're sorry, Mama. We'll do better." My sister attempted to comfort her.

"Just get out of my face, all of you!" my mother said in disgust.

No one else took a hit that night. My body broken, I limped to my room and crawled into bed. My welts seeped through the night so much that by morning my bed sheets stuck to my skin.

With so many fathers absent from households, single mothers simply repeated the cycle of corporal punishment passed down to them by their parents. They did the best they could, I suppose. It was all love, or so they said. In retrospect, it was my mother's rod that kept me on the right path. Where I lacked a consistent father figure, I had her to guide me, her and Mrs. Roberts. Like a bridge over troubled waters, the God that they both prayed to saw fit to save my life long enough for me to realize a potential that would take me far beyond G Street.

5 | Exit Strategy

As far as I could tell, there were three paths leading from G Street and out of the cycle of poverty: books, sports, and entertainment. Because I struggled in school, academics didn't seem like a realistic path for me. Sports were another pathway, but I lacked experience playing organized ball that stunted my development in the only sport that I truly loved. So I gravitated down the third path: entertainment.

I wasn't much of a dancer, but after years of the church choir, I could sing. Saturday mornings, I would stay glued to the TV, watching *Soul Train*, marveling at groups like the Stylistics, Shalamar, and the Silvers. Then I would spend a few more hours during the week in the mirror trying my best to imitate them. It was all preparation for what I imagined would be my big break: the talent show at Chollas Elementary School.

The talent show at Chollas was our *Showtime at the Apollo,* and the crowd was just as demanding. My big chance came in fifth grade when I took the stage as a solo act, sporting two-toned platform shoes and a powder-yellow denim suit. I pushed silver studs through the back of my jacket to read "Sunshine," the name of the song I performed by Earth, Wind, and Fire.

> Heavenly sunshine, only you can stop the rain
> Pouring in my heart, causing tears of pain.
> All of your feelin', seems to make me glow

Like beautiful sunshine that makes the flowers grow.

None of us could afford an instrumental version of the record. Looking every bit the star, I belted the lyrics over the top of EWF's record turned down low. My performance didn't make the huge splash that I thought it would. *What's wrong with these people? Didn't they just witness the next young Michael Jackson?* I received applause, but without a standing ovation, I felt as though my talent was under appreciated. I walked off the stage dejected.

A few minutes later, I found a seat in the audience and watched the rest of the show. The lineup included African boot dance ensembles, kids playing instruments, spoken word (although we didn't call it that back then), choreographed dance routines, and pitch-perfect renditions of songs by the Commodores, O'Jays, and Harold Melvin and the Blue Notes.

Wow, these kids are good, I thought as I sat in the audience watching the acts that came on after me. When a Samoan kid hit the high note in the climax of the song "Reasons" by Earth, Wind, and Fire, right then and there it dawned on me. In a neighborhood filled with talented kids, I was nothing special. My chances of being discovered as a singer were slim. Even so, being an entertainer or a professional athlete seemed more likely than becoming a college graduate.

My ambiguous relationship with the schoolhouse began when I lived on G Street. My mood and performance closely reflected my blood sugar. If my sugar was normal or high, I was animated, engaging, and otherwise acted like I had the good sense that God gave me. If my sugar was low, I bothered other kids, acted out, and talked back to teachers. My hypoglycemia and general lack of focus resulted in me being sent to the media and counseling center on a regular pass for a kind of detention, or more like an extended time-out. I sat in a cubicle and read a book or completed classroom worksheets. Usually, I would get around to what I loved doing the most: drawing pictures of the Road Runner and Wile E. Coyote for Pam, a student teacher.

Pam Perry is etched in my memory like *Dolly Madison.* She was high yellow in complexion with light brown eyes and sand-colored hair. The most beautiful thing around, her deep dimples and bright smile made me feel special. Whenever I was sent to the media center, she seemed to find me instantly. That was the best part of my extended time-outs. Pam was my silver lining. She had the power to turn my poor attitude around on a dime.

Pam eventually moved on. It would take years and many more time-outs and trips to detention before another teacher had any effect on me. The day it happened proved to be the most important experience of my elementary school years.

During my fifth-grade year, a substitute teacher took over my class for a few weeks. He was like no other teacher I had known not only because he was black but because he talked about how he was studying for dental school. Up until that point in my life, I had few positive black male role models to look up to or emulate, and I never had a male teacher. He was my hero immediately.

My new teacher taught my classmates and me the names of the teeth and how to count them. He taught us about basic dental hygiene and a lot of other fun things. From that point forward, I wanted to become a dentist. He was anxious to do something bigger than most people I had known, and I wanted to be like him. So I became genuinely interested in school for the first time.

Before my encounter with that man, I was another average black kid growing up in the hood: a fatherless, welfare-receiving, free-lunch-getting, happy-go-lucky black child without a single, concrete goal in sight. Making my way through the public school system, I was nobody special despite what Pam told me. Instead, I was headed nowhere in particular. Those few weeks of interacting with that substitute teacher altered my trajectory in life. A brief brush with his extraordinary ambition opened my world of possibilities.

FINISHER

It would be years from the time Smitty came and went before there was a man in the house to stabilize things, expanding my entire world, including our cramped living arrangement.

"How would you feel if Mom got married?" my mother asked all of us kids together.

Who finally stepped up to the plate? I wondered. My guess was the firefighter. He was a model type with a low-key demeanor and hands-off approach to parenting. He liked to chill, eat, and watch TV. He barely interacted with me, my brothers, and my sister. My prediction was off. Instead, my mother told us that she was considering marrying a former NFL veteran named Love. Despite the financial boost that marrying him would bring, I wasn't ready to share my mom.

"You don't have to get married, Mom. I can take care of you," I cried. My uncertain future became more uncertain, not less. *How will this man fit into our family? I'm too old to have to adapt to an in-house father now.* I figured that ship had sailed when Smitty left us. Eventually, I warmed up to the idea. Not that I had much of a choice. So 1977 became a year of milestones for me. My mom married Love Tolbert, and my family moved to the other side of town, leaving G Street far behind, and it was the year that I was finally allowed to play organized football.

Blended families are not easy. Embracing an outsider takes time. My stepdad, Jim, as we called him, may have been a nice companion for my mother, but he had some serious learning to do in the parenting department. That was clear from the start. Being a bachelor all of his life and not having any children of his own, gaining three teenagers and an eight-year-old imposed a steep learning curve for him and sometimes created tension. My brothers, my sister, and I stuttered and stumbled to find common ground on which to build individual relationships with our new stepfather. For me, this common ground began on the football field and grew from there. My bond with him evolved during our drives to and from Pop Warner football practices.

During that alone driving time with him, we discussed the finer points of being a defensive back, his former position in the NFL.

Jim dropped me off at practice with a few encouraging words, and I took off running toward the field, eager to put his advice to good use. Following practice, I looked forward to the drive home, discussing my performance, downing my Yoo-hoo chocolate drink, and munching on handfuls of trail mix. Jim drank his large Perrier water while he told me stories about his playing days. Eventually, Jim's care and loving tutelage would extend beyond the field of play. As far as the sport I loved, I looked up to him like that little boy in the 1970s Coca-Cola television commercial featuring Mean Joe Green. More important than that, because he showed wisdom, patience, temperance, responsibility, and friendship over the years, he grew into the father figure I needed. He demonstrated staying power and was the man that carried the baton across the finish line. I would come to love the man as the father that I never had.

BREAKTHROUGH

Groomed by the countless pick-up games on G Street, a few years of Pop Warner football, and tips from my new stepdad, I entered the tenth grade and tried out for the junior varsity football team. Five foot three inches as a fifteen-year-old, tipping the scales at 125 pounds dripping wet, I was undersized. Nonetheless, I was talented enough to start on both offense and defense. When football season ended, I wrestled at the 115-pound weight class. So as little as I was, I slimmed down even more after the football season to be pound-for-pound as strong as possible for wrestling. I wore a rubber suit underneath my sweats, spit a lot, and even threw up on occasion to achieve the lighter weight. Richard Simmons had nothing on me. I came home from practice famished. But rather than eating, I chewed on ice chips or sipped ice water with lemon slices. When I couldn't resist eating dinner or having dessert, I would eat and then immediately force it back up by sticking my finger down my throat.

"What are you doing?" Marvin would ask after hearing me behind the closed bathroom door.

Sweat beading on my forehead, I'd flush my dinner down the toilet and reassure him. "I'm all right, just not feeling too good," I'd say.

It was brutal and unhealthy. Although I earned a varsity letter for wrestling during my first year, it was little consolation. When the wrestling season ended, I went right into track season. With no eating restrictions (thank God!) my weight drifted back up. I ran intermediate hurdles and high hurdles and excelled at pole vaulting.

Each year, the cycle repeated. I would gain weight for football, lose weight for wrestling, and settle into my natural body weight during track season. Despite the merciless cycle, somehow I not only survived, but I also thrived. During my junior year, I played varsity in all three sports, earning captain honors in both football and wrestling. I was a high achiever, bar none. Our starting tailback on the football team, Clifford, outweighed me by nearly thirty pounds. It was unconventional to have a small guy as the fullback blocking for the bigger guy, but it worked. Coach Miller used to say, "You can fall forward for three yards," challenging me to find a way to gain short yardage. I ran hard, caught passes out of the backfield, and learned to fake handoffs so well that I'd get tackled on a regular basis.

Tackling opponents turned out to be far easier than tackling the books. At least that was the case as I was preparing to begin high school. Never a great student to begin with, I received unsatisfactory citizenship grades on my report cards for the first time. Then Ds and Fs followed closely behind. Detention took up more and more of my Saturdays, prompting Moms to have to go talk with my teachers often. As a new kid in a new neighborhood, attending a new school, I couldn't seem to maintain focus. Maybe I was bored, or maybe I was too preoccupied with my undersized stature. The kids at my new school were cruel. It wasn't long before they began calling me Inch-High Private Eye, the name of a popular cartoon at the time. Trying to make new friends while going through puberty was a lot for me to handle. It was about this time that Pam came into my life again.

Tracking me down somehow, she came to my house with a picture of a black man that I had drawn for her back in the day. She said that my picture was a good self-image. I wasn't sure what she meant by that, but her home visit boosted my self-esteem, if only for a short time.

Besides Pam, I rarely encountered teachers that inspired me. Ms. Augustine did capture my attention, for a minute at least. She taught English at Horace Mann Junior High. "A good essay should be like a lady's dress," she said wittily. "It should be long enough to cover all of the important parts but short enough to maintain interest." Pearls like that amused me, but for the most part, I went through the motions, uninspired with mediocre performances in all subjects until I received a letter in the tenth grade that changed everything.

> February 25, 1981
> Dear Lamar,
>
> Congratulations on achieving a 3.3 (or better) grade point average on your first-semester report card. Please share my pleasure in your academic success with your parents.
>
> Your grade point average makes you eligible for a place on the Principal's Honor Roll. If I can be of assistance to you in career or college planning, please stop in to see me.
>
> Sincerely,
> L. Young
> Counselor

College planning? Was that even a possibility for me? I couldn't figure out how I had performed so well, but the letter was proof positive that I could perform. A lightbulb went off. Suddenly, I saw myself as someone who could excel in school. *Maybe that could be my ticket to a better life. Not entertainment or sports but school.* I began to wonder if I could plot out another type of future for myself.

Determined to dedicate myself to the business of schoolwork, I'd tune the radio to a classical music station when I sat down at home to read. My trips to the library to get a head start on my homework before the morning bell rang became more frequent. Before long, I became the one providing answers to test questions instead of the one asking for them. With renewed dedication, I turned the corner academically and began to excel in my schoolwork as well as sports. In my mind at least, I had become a double threat. When the dust settled, I earned seven varsity letters in three years and finished in the top 20 percent of my graduating class, earning my way onto the Principal's Honor Roll five of the six semesters.

During my senior year, I went on to win several wrestling tournaments and became the first California Interscholastic Federation wrestling champion in my high school's twenty-five-year history. A two-way starter on the football team, I played strong safety and earned Most Outstanding Defensive Back honors. Somewhere along the way, I even managed to sit for the Scholastic Aptitude Test. I didn't study for the SAT or take a review course for the exam. Instead, I showed up one Saturday morning unprepared, holding a handful of number-two pencils with an undeserved swagger. My counselor encouraged me to sit for the test. She also sent my name to a recruiter for the University of California at Berkeley, a place I hadn't even heard of before then.

Following my final football game of the regular season, I stood gathered among other players and fans in the school parking lot. It was dark and cold. But the pending news was worth it as we waited with bated breath for Coach to take the official phone call. Suddenly, Coach Miller pushed open his office door to deliver the news, with a smile overtaking his customarily stern face.

"We're in!" he announced.

We all went crazy. Players and students hugged each other with joy, celebrating the fact that we were in the playoffs for the first time in more than ten years. So happy just to play a post-season game in front of a capacity crowd under the Friday-night lights, I thought that would be the highlight of my senior year. That was before I received the news I had been anxiously awaiting.

PART 2
HIGHER
LEARNING

6 | Misguided

My academic turnaround put me in a position to apply for college. With a few things to offer, including a strong GPA and a good record of extracurricular activities, I had a decent chance of getting into somewhere respectable. My ridiculously low combined SAT score of around 880 left plenty of room for doubt. It wasn't as though I reviewed for the test or even studied for it. Turned out that going into the test cold wasn't the best idea after all.

The University of California at Berkeley, called Cal for short, was the only place that I applied to for admission. If I had slept in on the Saturday of orientation with Berkeley recruiters, an appointment arranged by my high school counselor, I would have missed the opportunity altogether. Before meeting the recruiter, I hadn't even heard of the school. As fate would have it, one application was enough. Cal accepted me on my record, and I entered as a member of the freshman class of 1983. My prayers were answered. At the time I entered college, my mother hadn't attended college, although she had earned her GED. My stepdad left college early for the NFL. My sister withdrew from college after a few incomplete semesters at two different schools, and my older brother, LaSalle, spent the better part of his high school years at an alternative high school. So when it came to me attending college, it was neither assumed nor expected. If I went and graduated, I would be the first to do so in my family. Either way, I was headed for uncharted territory.

My first exposure to college life was during weekend orientation, called Cal Student Orientation, or CalSO for short. Unwilling to give up my last summer in sunny San Diego to attend the longer six-week summer bridge program as hundreds of entering freshman students did, I was willing to invest a single weekend. During orientation, I stayed in the dorms, learned study skills, toured the campus, and preregistered for classes. But by far the most exciting part of this early exposure was the taste of independence.

By the second day of orientation, I connected with a young woman. A graduate from an all-girls Catholic school in Los Angeles, Linda had led a rather sheltered life according to her report. That night we sat up talking in the common lounge of our dorm for hours on end, staring at each other on the eve of our university experience and the first extended time away from home. The sun came up, and we continued to talk. The only thing that saved us from ourselves was Parents' Day the next morning; she went back to her room to prepare for her mother, who came up to check on her. I staggered back to my room to get some much-needed sleep. Linda and I hooked up Sunday night for an all-night petting session.

"Be careful out there. You know what I mean? Take precautions. There are a lot of diseases going around, and you don't want to get caught up," my stepdad cautioned when he dropped me at the airport days earlier.

As I reflected back to my birds-and-bees talk with Jim, it occurred to me that neither Linda nor I was in any big rush. We had years to get to know each other. There was nothing threatening our future love affair. There was only time and opportunity. We said our good-byes the next morning, sealed it with a kiss, and promised each other that we'd pick up right where we left off when school officially began three weeks later.

Linda was my first college sweetheart, or so I thought. Despite the flowers and cards that I sent her, she wouldn't even return my calls when school began. I tried for weeks before giving up on her. The cold fact of the matter was I went and fell in love, but she wasn't feeling me once school began. So overcome by her newfound freedom, Linda went buck-wild. Six weeks into the first semester, as a result of her binge drinking, she was hospitalized for alcohol poisoning and had to have her stomach pumped as a life-saving measure. By all reports, binging episodes occurred repeatedly, and she quickly gained the reputation of being a wild party girl, becoming a poster child for what not to do with the newfound freedoms of college life.

Unlucky in love, my studies became my primary focus, but I had some nagging concerns. What troubled me most was the pitifully small number of African American students on campus. Some black students would joke that you could go an entire day without seeing another black person. I knew Berkeley wasn't Howard University, but for a school with the motto "Excellence in Diversity," this was a problem. Of course it wasn't quite that bad, but when I stepped into the larger lecture halls, seating hundreds of students, I often felt like I was the last of the Mohicans. It was a hollow, desperate kind of a feeling to enter those lecture halls with almost paralyzing apprehension. Each time I'd walk through the door, I'd immediately look around for other dark faces that resembled my own. It wasn't as if I would become instant friends or study partners with the other black and brown students, but I felt comfort in numbers. For me, there was a grim anxiety that came with being the only token black student in the class—like I walking a tightrope for the first time without a net.

Despite feeling anxious and out of place in certain circumstances, I had a positive feeling knowing that Cal was an incubator for opportunities, or so it seemed. Everywhere I looked, people were carrying backpacks bulging with books. Students scuttled here and there trying to get something that could never be taken away: an education. Still in disbelief of actually making it into Cal, the overarching Sather Gate, the white marble of Sproul (Biko) Plaza, the weathered wood benches that sat in Dwinelle Plaza, and the sweet, melodious concerts that rang out from the Campanile Bell Tower seemed to call to me: welcome to Cal.

College was a time of internal awakenings. For instance, when I began college, I discovered that I had no sense of personal style.

When it came to dressing, the muscle T-shirts that I sported in high school weren't making much of a fashion statement at the university, especially since my muscles weren't all that developed. So I used some of my financial-aid money to improve my wardrobe. I invested in Cole Haan penny loafers, turtlenecks from the GAP, cardigan sweaters, and logo-laden college sweatshirts. Preppy was the style of the day, so I tried my best to dress like a college man and look the part.

Desperately trying not to fit in, I made bleach-splattered motifs on my blue jeans and denim jackets, cut several lines of different lengths into the side of my hair, and even sported a little tail at the nape of my neck, bleached with over-the-counter hydrogen peroxide. In a bold, thoughtless action of independence, I shaved the entire right side of my head. It was a confusing time of my life, and I tried my best not to disappear into a white world. Inspired yet somewhat overwhelmed by it all, to attempt both to fit in and not fit in created a sort of schism of being—too cool to ask for advice, and too naïve to practice sound judgment. Striving for independence and conformity, all at the same time, resulted in my stumbling. As a seventeen-year-old freshman, I still had much to learn about college life.

THE SESSION

I received one of my first big lessons the day I made an appointment with a guidance counselor for some direction. Even though I had no idea what I would need in the way of coursework to apply to medical school, I remained determined to follow in the footsteps of my fifth-grade teacher and be a health professional. After waiting patiently in the reception area of the wooden bungalows that we called the T-buildings, I was delighted to see that the counselor assigned to me was a black man. *What! What were the chances of that happening? I lucked out.* As it turned out, my excitement was short-lived. I quickly learned that not every black man is down for the cause or in your corner.

I introduced myself. "Hi. I'm LaMar Hasbrouck, an incoming freshman," I said.

After we had shaken hands, I sat my brand-new Jansport backpack on the floor beside me, took a seat in front of him, and began to share my goal to attend medical school. His response was quick and quite unexpected. Rather than try to work with me, he immediately broke into what I can only describe as a doomsday sermon. He was subtle at first.

"Well, if you want to go to medical school, you'll need a 3.5 GPA or better. And that includes the science courses," he lectured.

Then he rattled off the percentage of students who applied to medical school each year but failed to get in.

"Lots of students don't make it in. There are about six or seven student applications for every one available spot," he continued.

With an air of self-importance and total lack of compassion, he described how I would have to make any number of sacrifices to have any chance at all of getting into med school. Hanging onto every word he said, I simply nodded. Occasionally he flipped through the catalog of classes or pretended to move important files from one side of his desk to the other. Every so often, he eyeballed me to check for my reaction. My discomfort began to swell into anger as it was apparent to me that I would not get the guidance I needed from this black man. My heart sank when I came to the realization that I was wasting his time.

"Okay," I replied, nodding sheepishly, my palms sweating.

Finally, he looked me square in the face and spoke the words that I will never forget. He said, "Maybe you should think about doing something other than going to medical school." Translation: you ain't never going to go to no medical school.

Did I hear him correctly? This fool doesn't know me from a can of paint. It was only the third week of school, for God's sake. Hell, I had barely begun my coursework. Who's to say I wouldn't be a straight-A student? Was that his notion of counseling?

The irony of the situation was that in some warped way he probably thought he was doing me a favor by directing me down the path of least resistance. He obviously thought very little of my capabilities and almost certainly didn't want me to attempt to set the bar high. Just thirty minutes before our encounter, I was elated, believing that he would help to jump-start my dreams. Instead, he tried to invalidate them. Truth be told, he attempted to cancel them altogether. A few more pep talks from him, and I would have been well on my way to dropping out of Cal and enlisting in the armed forces or enrolling in a trade school. I vowed that he would never see my black face again. As I descended the stairs leaving the building, my spirit was down, but my head was held high as I resolved to succeed despite him.

My dream died a little bit on that day. I wondered how many other black and brown students he had misguided. It was no wonder that so many of us walked around campus filled with insecurities. Counselors like him in positions to encourage us unconsciously conspired to defeat and denigrate us. Even at age seventeen, I had sense enough to know that much. He was the delusional one, not me. In his estimation, I may have been just another black kid who rode in on an affirmative action program, but I refused to believe that I was in over my head. Determined, I wasn't going to allow that fool to slam the door shut on my dream.

7 | Griffiths Hall

Growing up at 4497 G Street, I lived under a flat, rectangular, gravel-covered roof, surrounded by a three-foot-high chain-linked fence. It was the house that my mother grew up in as a child and then rented from my grandparents for fifty-five dollars a month. Some nights the four of us would stay up in our tiny room for hours sharing. LaSalle would talk about the bike he fixed or the go-cart he was in the process of building. Marvin, our little neighborhood mayor, would tell about the new friends he made or divulge the rumors he'd overheard. I recounted the jar full of bees I caught, pulling wings off bugs, or the latest experiment I conducted. And little mama would lament her frustration about the cake that fell because she opened the oven too many times.

Then we'd close out the night much like the popular sitcom of that era, *The Waltons*:

"Good night, Jaeneen," I'd say.

"Good night, LaMar," she'd say in return.

"Good night, LaSalle."

"Good night, Marvin," and so forth, all short of the "Good night, John-boy" line made so popular by that 1970s television series.

SUSTENANCE

Government cheese and powdered eggs flowed like milk and honey through every household on G Street. And just like the federal care package was common for families on my block, so too was the free school meal plan. Every kid attending my elementary school received free breakfast and lunch. Trust me. I came to depend upon those meals because I seldom ate breakfast at home during the week. The cereal that Moms bought was reserved for the weekends. Some mornings I'd arrive on time for school but too late for breakfast. My heart dropped into my empty stomach every time I rushed into the cafeteria, hoping I could grab something, if only a carton of chocolate milk. Late, I'd look around to find discarded milk and juice cartons scattered everywhere and see kids being dismissed to class. It was only my fear of embarrassment that prevented me from snatching up those half-eaten ham and egg turnovers and dashing off to class.

On one occasion, the temptation of food was almost too strong for me to resist. My mother had a girlfriend named Joanne that would keep us for a few hours after school until Moms got off of work. Far too often, Joanne would call her kids in for dinner and leave us outside playing in the dirt, usually without as much as a snack. One afternoon, she threw out a pan of Jiffy cornbread into a large trash can that sat alongside the house without a lid on it. Within minutes, I worked my way over to that trash can and suddenly found myself standing over those steaming yellow pieces of broken bread. Just as I was about to reach for them, I heard the most annoying voice.

"Eww! You're eating out of the trash can! He's eating out of the trash can!"

It was Joanne's youngest daughter. Thanks to her outing me, I never actually ate out of the trash can, but I certainly would have dumpster dived if she hadn't blown the whistle. The truth is I was hungry.

If necessity is the mother of invention, then hunger is the mother of creative snacking. Snacks included butter and sugar sandwiches, mayonnaise toast, peanut butter on a spoon, peppermint sticks in lemons, and syrup on a plate. No pancakes. I poured syrup onto a plate, imagined that I was finishing up a big stack of pancakes, and licked it clean. When you grow up in a family struggling to make ends meet, food can become a central focus in your life. Every now and again, I would attempt to hide food in our empty refrigerator. It was no easy task stashing food in places like a bag of flour or behind the produce drawer. Sometimes I was successful, and sometimes one of my hungry siblings would find my stash and eat it.

GOOD EATS

Living in the university dorms, or residence halls as they're called nowadays, was worlds apart from my early beginnings on G Street. Griffiths Hall, located on a plot called Unit 2, was my assigned dorm. It was a small housing complex with four high-rise buildings, each facing a common courtyard. The small rooms had space for two beds, two dressers, and a portable fridge but not much else. It didn't bother me because I was used to tight quarters growing up. The cafeteria was located in the center of the courtyard and quickly became a regular stop for me throughout the day. Coming from G Street, where a good meal was scarce, I looked forward to the food in the cafeteria. Dorm food was like a taste explosion. For example, I had never tasted a bagel with cream cheese before then. That was exactly what my taste buds craved, something different. *So this is what Jewish people eat.*

When I walked through the line in the cafeteria, I felt like a king. Breakfast choices included pancakes and waffles, scrambled eggs and omelets made to order, sausage, bacon, corn beef hash (something else I had never tried before then), home-fried potatoes, hot cereal, and the list went on and on. There was also a full juice bar, a cereal bar, fruit, yogurt, cottage cheese, and whole, skimmed, and chocolate milk. It was good eats. As an active, skinny kid, it was important for me to have access to that much food. The higher the fat and the higher carbohydrate diet, the better.

Dorm assignments were a source of anxiety because I had no idea who I'd end up with for a roommate. The thought of sharing tight quarters with someone you couldn't get along with was cause for heartburn, but I lucked out. Rick quickly became my boy. A Mexican brother from Stockton, California, we were paired up based on a dorm room compatibility survey. Go figure. We had similar tastes in music. We were both self-professed pre-med majors, although no such major existed at Berkeley. And we were both from working-class blended families with stepdads. We hit it off famously. Rick and I got along so well that I was borrowing his car to take girls out by the end of the semester and riding with him to Stockton on the weekends to pick up stacks of homemade flour tortillas his mom would make as part of his care package. More than thirty years later, we are still friends.

Rick moved out of the dorm after one semester. He found a room for rent in a house nearby. He had an opportunity to save a lot of money, so he grabbed it. I couldn't begrudge him that. His replacement was this goofy white boy that pressed my nerves and made me work hard to tolerate him. Tall, pale, with a bad complexion and no social life to speak of, Rick's replacement cramped my style. It seemed like every time I came back to the room, he was there, just chilling. It would have been different to find a rubber band on the doorknob, the universal signal that he had a girl in the room. But that was not the case. My roomie didn't have it like that. He was more like a lounge dweller. So my bringing a girlie back to the room was out of the question. Talk about losing cool points. As a result, my stuttering social life took place outside of my dorm room.

There were other problems with my new roomie besides my inability to bring by female visitors. For one, my food kept turning up missing from our little fridge. Two, he had a little foot odor problem. But the biggest problem was that he also had an issue with my singing. I don't mean to brag, but back in the day, I had a falsetto that allowed me to hit almost any high note. I remember singing the climactic bridge to the song "Slow Jam" by Midnight Star:

> Won't you play another slow jam …
> Woo, woo-oo-oo, please Mr. DJ.

Unlike Rick, my new roommate wasn't feeling my soulful crooning.

"Uh, LaMar … would you mind? Could you please not sing out loud?" he asked.

I continued to sing anyhow. The more I sang, the more he protested. Finally, I had to put my foot down. "Look, man. Half the dorm room is mine. If I want to sing in my half of the room, then I'm going to sing," I said, running out of patience.

Eventually, we came to a place of understanding. I sang. He wore his headphones. We gradually warmed up to each other and managed to make it through the semester without a major incident.

COEDS

The coed dorm setup was mind-blowing. At least that's what my parents thought after coming out to visit me. One floor was all female, and another was all male. The remaining eight floors were coed. Girls and boys on the coed floors shared everything. We shared a common lounge. We used the same showers and sinks. We even took turns using the same bathroom stalls. I'm not going to lie. At first it was awkward walking into a shower immediately after your female neighbor walked out clad in only a shower cap, towel, and flip-flops. But after seeing everyone a few times in every possible scenario, the shock eventually wore off.

It wasn't long before I hooked up with a young lady who lived in my building. Her roommate went home nearly every weekend. It was a beautiful thing. She also lived on a coed floor, four stories above me, on the eighth. Kelly was six foot two and the color of caramel. She was small up top and heavier toward the bottom. She had wavy black hair, the face of an angel, and a playful sense of humor. Her stature was impressive, but the thing that was most alluring to me was her quiet confidence. Inside her Amazonian frame was a young woman demure and unassuming. Rarely do you find beauty so striking that it makes you dizzy, but Kelly had that effect on me. In fact, she was the kind of girl who drove the boys on the yard bonkers. Muscle-headed football players were particularly impressed by her and clearly underwhelmed with her choice to hang with me. They probably felt that a woman with her physical attributes was best suited for someone six foot something and two hundred-plus pounds. It burned them up that she was down with a brother like me, a little guy. They didn't have to worry for long. As sweet as our time spent was, Kelly transferred to another school a year later. We weren't officially a couple, so we didn't officially break up. We simply lost touch with each other. At the time, I didn't even know where she went. With the abrupt ending of that special friendship, it was up to me to find another hobby, and that didn't take too long.

Movies playing on campus at Wheeler Hall, arcades and bowling in the basement of the Student Union Center, fraternity parties, pep rallies, dances, dating, drinking, and more. The list of possibilities for a college student away from home was endless. The real trick was not getting too far sucked into the distractions that you forgot the reason you were at school to begin with. We have all heard the stories about students who successfully crossed the burning sands into a fraternity, for example, yet never earned their college degree. I did my level best to enjoy the social offerings of Berkeley and stay on task.

Griffiths Hall had an interesting cast of characters on the fourth floor in 1983. Directly across the hall from Rick and me were two white guys. Dan was from money, as best I could tell. His father was an architect. His roommate, Mike, was a budding journalist and absolute sports fanatic. Mike worked his way up to sports editor for the university newspaper, the *Daily Californian*. Years later, he'd go on to become a professional sports writer, working for *ESPN* magazine and Yahoo Sports.

Mike and Dan kept their room door open and blasted music into the hallway almost nonstop. They probably had no clue that they might be offending others on the floor with their brand of music. They just took it upon themselves to be the hallway deejays. While living in Griffiths Hall, I came to learn something about white boys or white folks in general. They can sometimes feel a sense of entitlement. I certainly didn't appreciate their music in the beginning, but I genuinely liked the dudes personally, so I was open to trying something different. They weren't the kind of bands I grew up imitating from Soul Train, but it wasn't all bad. In the end, thanks to them, I learned to appreciate artists like the Cars, Squeeze, and Joe Jackson. I learned to love songs like "Alison" by Elvis Costello and the Attractions:

> Alison, I know this world is killing you.
> Oh, Alison, my aim is true.

Our two resident hall celebrities, Terrence, who we called T-Mac, and Big Mel, lived to the left of Mike and Dan. They were scholarship football players, both running backs and the only ballers in our entire dorm. T-Mac was from a 5-A high school in Beaumont, Texas. Mel played his high school ball somewhere in Bakersfield, California. Both were heavily recruited. The entire dorm, especially Mike, seemed to live vicariously through them. Those two were our window into big-time college ball. I was not big time, not even close. When I entered Cal, I did so without the slightest inclination to play college ball. But after attending my first football game, it wasn't long before I found myself daydreaming about that very possibility.

8 | True Colors

"Hey, nigger!"

The day I heard those words, I felt it like a fist in my gut. It was a crisp fall day in Northern California. The entire campus was abuzz with excitement for the first game of the 1983 football season. Cal was coming off an average season the year before but during the final game of the season had engineered what would go down as one of the greatest endings in college football history, a performance that became known as *The Play*. It was the last play of the last game in the 1982 season closer against Cal's bitter rival, Stanford. The Big Game, as it is called, was more about pride than anything else. The game came down to four seconds. Four Cal players tossed the ball five times during the kickoff return. The final ball carrier, who was also the first to receive the kickoff, ran for a touchdown through the Stanford band that had run onto the field early to celebrate. It turned out to be premature as the Cal player knocked down the final Stanford "defender," a trombone player, and snatched victory from John Elway's Stanford team. With a season finale like that, Cal fans couldn't wait for the opening game of the 1983 season against San Jose State, a non-conference opponent. Cal was in the Pacific-10 Athletic Conference with UCLA, USC, Stanford, Oregon, Oregon State, Washington State, Arizona, Arizona State, and Washington. Few sports are as big as Division I-A football on a college campus. And Cal was no exception.

It was my first college football game, and I was so ready to kick off what I knew would be an exciting season. At that time, I knew nothing about The Play or Cal football. Nonetheless, I was excited and anxious to find my place in the student section along with the tens of thousands of other fanatics. With my roommate, Rick, I made my way to Memorial Stadium, winding up hills, through the streets, past dorms and fraternity houses. It seemed like the entire campus and city of Berkeley was going to the game. To call it festive would be an understatement. Like ants marching up an anthill, people migrated to the stadium from a hundred different directions.

Along Greek row, fraternities sold beer from kegs right on their front lawns. I was never a drinker, but I thought to myself, *I'm a college man now. Why not?* That cold cup of beer, the sun shining on my face, and the music of laughter, chatter, and grand expectations made my walk to the student section unbelievable. A legitimate part of the college scene, I was a long way from the small world of G Street. There I was in the excitement, wearing my Cal colors. Seventeen, healthy, strong, and energetic, I was invincible. It was confusing, maddening, and invigorating all at once. I didn't know quite what to expect. Like a leaf swept up by a strong wind, I was lifted toward the stadium with thousands of other students, faculty, and alumni. My eyes must have looked like saucers. With my heart pounding, I continued to march.

Finally, I pushed through the turnstile and found my spot among the masses. Crowded like a sardine in a can, I was a happy camper in a sea of blue and gold. I watched the spectacle of cheerleaders and the Cal mascot, Oski. Then the cannon sounded, and the teams ran out of a tunnel and onto the field. I was pumped. I had never attended a college football game in my life. And there I was watching *my* team run onto the field. The crowd was rowdy. Occasionally they would break out into a chant directed at some spectator or student wearing even a speck of red, the color of Stanford: "Take off that red shirt! Take off that red shirt …"

It would begin with a few voices and within minutes, seconds really, swell into a condemning ruckus with hundreds, even thousands, of voices with indignant fingers pointing at the perpetrator. It was a call with one purpose: shaming the student into taking off the item. When they did, the crowd went wild with applause. Sometimes the poor soul would physically get rolled up, hand-over-head all the way up the student section and out of the stands. It was a rock concert mentality. And I joined the chorus.

"Roll him up ... roll him up." It was contagious.

Boom! The cannon sounded again. It was time for the halftime show. The Cal marching band came high-stepping out of the tunnel through a cloud of smoke. They were too clean in their dark blue military uniforms, caps with white plumes, black shoes with crisp white spats.

"Tuba, tuba, tuba," the crowd chanted as the sousaphones broke formation to freestyle across the field.

At some point during the halftime show, the cheerleaders, perched on a platform near the players' bench area, instructed us to look under our seats. Everyone in the student section had a large colored card with blue on one side and gold on the other. I held mine overhead and flipped it on cue to spell out the word Cal in gold script letters on a background of blue. On command, I flipped it again, and we spelled out the same in reverse colors. It was a fitting tribute to the alumni sitting in their section of the bleachers across the field from us. Afterward, all the students threw their cards into the air like caps on graduation day. Then the chant began: "You know it. You tell the story. You tell the whole damn world this is Bear Territory!" The crowd sang out. We must have repeated that chant a hundred times during a three-hour game. My voice was nearly hoarse from all my cheering for Cal. In the end, I cheered my team to victory, along with 45,000 other fans.

Boom! The cannon sounded for the final time, ending the contest. Cal won the game 30–9, and I was thrilled.

Whoa. What a blast! I thought as I began my walk back to Griffith Hall along with thousands of other keyed-up students and fans making their way back to their homes. I didn't bother with a second beer. Tipsy from the whole fan experience, I couldn't get any higher.

"Hey, nigger!" a voice rang out.

Did I hear what I thought I heard? I looked around to find the source of the voice.

"Yeah you, nigger. I'm talking to you."

Then I spotted him. It was some ignorant white boy hanging out of a window at one of the fraternity houses. Pop. Just that quickly, my bubble broke as my near-perfect day abruptly ended.

I have always been a person aware of both my race and my surroundings. Never for a minute was it lost on me that I was a black man at a predominantly white university. But oddly enough, on that day, at that moment, being black was the farthest thing from my mind. If I was any color, I was blue and gold. Unfortunately, even in a sea of smiling, jubilant faces bonded by victory, I was reminded otherwise. Powerless, I was embarrassed and ashamed. My shame was not about who I was. My shame was because I was so vulnerable that I allowed a racist comment to penetrate my soul, steal my joy, and break my spirit. It would take me years to develop a thick skin and coping strategies for those types of attacks.

There were other signs of racism on campus. Like the time when a group of drunken frat boys threw a beer bottle through my dorm room window. True, I probably shouldn't have yelled out the window for them to keep it down, but I would hardly call that provocation for violence. When I told T-Mac and Mel what happened, they were ready to throw down.

"They did what? How come you didn't get us?" Mel asked.

I guess I was so shaken after dodging the flying beer bottle and shattered glass that it never occurred to me to get reinforcements and go after them. It was probably better that I didn't get them involved. That incident could have turned real ugly real quick, especially given the fact that alcohol was involved. They could have lost their football scholarships, and folks could have gotten seriously injured. The whole thing happened so fast, leaving me almost baffled about the entire ordeal. In my immediate recounting of the events, I wasn't quite sure what had prompted me to yell out of the window in the first place. Was I subconsciously acting out as a result of what had been done to me? But that was months earlier. I did not yell racial slurs or call those white boys out of their name. But there I was, perched safely in my dorm room window, four stories above the street, yelling at folks minding their own business. If they were a group of young black men, would I have said a word? Maybe, but I doubt it. In some odd sense, that truth made me no better than the frat boy that ruined my perfect football Saturday afternoon. That caused a shame of a different sort.

9 | Daylight

After only one semester, my shortcomings as a student were glaring, even to me. My misguidance counselor, as bleak a picture as he painted, was correct about one thing: my academic success would be a steep climb and would require the best of my efforts. I lacked college-educated parents who could guide me through the process of choosing classes, tell me how best to study, or advise me about something as simple as time management. To make matters worse, I failed the college entrance exam for English. Because I was at an academic disadvantage, I was compelled to rely on my vision.

The vision I created was based on the simple reasoning that the determining factor for obtaining a college degree was getting in, and I had done that. I was rubbing shoulders with some of the best and brightest students from across the country and the world. The students that entered Cal seemed to have a real sense of purpose. They were emboldened by the very real prospect of becoming doctors, lawyers, mathematicians, engineers, professors, or anything else they envisioned. They were admitted. All they had left to do was to choose a career path, pass their courses, and presto, they were in the position to have their piece of the American dream. If they were captains of their destiny, why couldn't I be too? I was enrolled just as they were.

So I adopted that mind-set and figured I, too, could be whatever I wanted to be. I decided I was going to become a medical doctor. The trick was to find a way to stay in college and finish the coursework that could lead me there. I had to survive the social and academic rigors of school for my dream to endure.

For my first semester, I put together a simple course of study that included an introductory philosophy course, Chemistry P, Math P, and something called Subject A. The P stood for preparation. Subject A was remedial English. I recognized that I was not strong enough to take introductory math or chemistry, so I took preparatory courses for each. To be honest, I was completing high school and starting college simultaneously. Because I had a good sense of myself, I was not about to be blown out of the water during my first year. My objective was to survive, even if that meant starting slow. Survive to fight another day; that was the plan.

My plan wasn't fail-proof, but it was a place to start. I would like to tell you that I sailed through my courses with flying colors. I would like to tell you that, but that wouldn't be true. Those classes weren't easy for me, and I suffered plenty. It took me some time to get my academic legs under me. The sad awakening was that I had no idea how far behind or unprepared I was. For example, I used a highlighter for the first time. I remember how cool I thought it was to light up text in a book with a yellow marker and to be able to read the words underneath. Of course, I was never allowed to write in my schoolbooks before college, but in college, writing in your books was encouraged. The difference was you bought your books, so you owned them. In the beginning, I highlighted everything. There was more highlighted text than I left un-highlighted. I didn't know what I was doing.

Much of my college behavior was mimicking what I thought I should be doing to be successful. Most students, including me, were too afraid to admit what they didn't know. The problem is that you often don't know what you don't know. It took me a few semesters to become a good highlighter. It took me longer still to develop a study style that would get me through my courses with reasonable success. Before getting the knack of it, I spent too many late nights studying until the morning, pulling all-nighters. Some students needed to consume coffee or take caffeine tablets to pull all-nighters. Not me. I was able to make it on my natural adrenaline that came from the fear of failing.

I'd say to myself, *I can learn this stuff,* or *I can figure out what's going to be on the test tomorrow.* Who was I fooling? More often than not, I guessed wrong. But that kind of mental game playing got me through many winding nights of playing catch-up. In truth, I probably ended up doing marginally better than I would have if I had just thrown in the towel and gotten a good night's sleep. Of course, regular studying during the semester would have been by far the best strategy for success. The all-nighter method of studying is not recommended. Based on this better-late-than-never approach, what I can say is that I never walked into a test thinking that I was going to bomb the exam outright. I believed in the words of Helen Keller, "A true soldier does not acknowledge defeat before the battle." So I fought. At times, I fought to learn weeks of material overnight.

SUBJECT A

For those that couldn't write, remedial English composition, called Subject A, was mandatory. Unfortunately, I was among them. The course was a nightmare. There were no tests. There were only essays. There were lots and lots of essays. My instructor for the course tried to destroy my spirit. She had me feeling like I couldn't put together a complete sentence. A few weeks into the course, I had serious doubts that English was my first language. That woman was downright evil to me. I couldn't figure out what I did to offend her, but she had it in for me from the start. She marked up my papers so much that my compositions bled with red ink. The harder I tried to write well, the harsher her criticism, it seemed. She would call me into her office for no other purpose than to belittle me. Or at least that's how I felt. On more than one occasion, I nearly came to tears.

For whatever reason, that middle-aged, overweight woman was hell-bent on riding my jockstrap. Maybe she believed, as my counselor did, that I didn't belong at Berkeley. I endured her for the entire semester, working my ass off trying to please her first and master English composition second. And for the entire semester, she never murmured a single word of encouragement. Not one. Miraculously, by the end of the semester, I earned a C grade. Elated, I was never happier earning a passing grade, and I put both the course and the instructor behind me.

As my studying progressed, I became a solitary creature. Some students seemed to thrive in study groups with three or more persons. But I preferred to study alone. To me, study groups were a colossal waste of time. They were irritating. The idea was that each person in the study group learned one section of the assignment well. Each member would then do his or her best to teach that portion of the material to the others in the group. Divide and conquer was the model. This strategy prevented one person from having to carefully study the entire assignment. Unfortunately, student reviews typically turned out to be one big dog and pony show. There are few things more maddening to me than a room full of self-professed experts. As the group learning progressed, each presenter was more obnoxious than the one before. Sometimes attending student-run study groups was a really good way to become even more confused about a given subject. Good learners didn't always make good teachers. I would end up wanting to choke at least one of my classmates by the time the group session ended. I quickly learned to avoid those pseudo-social gatherings.

Instead of study groups, I took a learn-as-you-go-along approach to my education. I chose my courses based on word of mouth and my personal interests. Admittedly, I was a little gun-shy to engage in formal guidance counseling after my initial experience. But I knew that to stay alive academically I would have to reach out for help eventually.

In the meantime, I volunteered to add football tryouts to my load. The confidence that I had in my ability to perform in the classroom when I entered Cal was fading fast. Sports, on the other hand, were like an old friend that would never forsake me. The gridiron always felt like home, and I wanted to be a player, not just a fan. My drive was strong, but I didn't quite know why. Maybe I desired validation, or possibly I longed to be evaluated in a different way. For whatever reason, I was compelled to take that test.

PART 3
BIG TIME

10 | Walk-On

Having a competitive streak and the ability to juke speeding cars and scale tall buildings back on G Street prepared me for the greatest game ever played in my world: football. For years prior, I suffered in silence watching the neighborhood kids come home from practice in their grass-stained football pants. They'd walk down G Street holding helmets draped with shirted shoulder pads. In those days, there were few famous African American NFL players for me to admire. So you can imagine how I burned with envy looking at those battle-tested warriors wearing OJ Simpson cleats. The bright orange bottoms of their cleats seemed to hold magical powers. If only I had a pair, I was certain that I could run like The Juice. My mom was dead-set against me playing contact sports at nine years old, and I couldn't understand why. Like every other kid in the neighborhood, I longed to play football for Valencia Park (VP), the local Pop Warner powerhouse that practiced on the field at legendary Lincoln High School. Lincoln wasn't only where my mom and Lee went to school. More importantly, Marcus Allen, who later became an NFL Hall of Fame running back, and his younger brother, Damon, a star in the Canadian Football League, played for Lincoln.

It was years before I discovered the real reason my mom refused my pleas. She always told my older brother and me that she couldn't locate our birth certificates, which was a far stretch from the truth but a requirement to sign up. As a struggling single mom of four, it shouldn't have come as a shock to me to learn the real reason I couldn't play was because we lacked health insurance. Bottom line, my mother paid all of our medical bills out of pocket, and she literally could not afford for me to get hurt.

If I had known the real reason at the time, it would have been hard for me to wrap my mind around it. I thought myself invincible, incapable of suffering from a broken bone or torn ligament. I wore Sears Toughskins jeans with the reinforced patch over my knees. If my mom had given me a chance to prove myself, my thought would have been, *Mom, you will never have to worry about money or health insurance again.* I *was* The Juice. That never happened, of course. I pleaded for a chance to play. My mom refused, relentlessly. I had to find another way to prove myself on the field, settling for pickup games on the front lawn of Chollas Elementary School.

There were no parks nearby, so I was forced to play on a narrow sprinkler-riddled stretch of grass on school property, located on the corner of Market and Forty-Ninth Street, just a stone's throw from my house. The advantage of the sprinkler heads at Chollas Elementary was that we could siphon off a cool drink of water when dying of thirst. The downside was risking a busted kneecap or chipped tooth on the metal sprinkler heads. I managed to avoid chipping a tooth but regularly sprained my ankles, busted my lip, bit my tongue, and tore open my knees and elbows.

When it came to picking playground teams, Wayne was usually the first little guy chosen. He was small like me, but unlike me, he had Pop Warner experience. He played for VP and had a reputation as someone with blazing speed and quickness. As time went on, I developed my reputation as a player that never shied away from a collision. I tackled much bigger players, even if it meant being dragged across the goal line gripping their shoelaces. If I had to take a knee to the lip to bring someone down twice my size, I did. Wayne, on the other hand, avoided contact at all cost. If he could not outrun you or out-juke you, he was in deep trouble. He was fast, very fast, but he was soft as cotton candy. For that reason, as time went by, I surpassed him in the neighborhood draft.

"I'll take my man right here," the older boys said, pointing to me. My small chest swelled with pride.

I was eleven and at the peak of my glory days on G Street, and the older boys ranged from twelve to sixteen years old. We played four-on-four or five-on-five, depending on how many folks we could round up. The moment the ball went up in the air, it was on. Eight or ten kids looking like Fat Albert's gang ran toward each other at top speed like titans. Elbows were flying, Keds tennis shoes striking the ground, knees churning; we collided with the force of ten boys on their rite of passage, playing straight-up hard-nosed tackle football. If I got the ball on a kickoff return, which was thrown, not kicked, I ran for daylight, scrambling, twisting, and struggling for a few extra feet. I played bigger than my body. I played game after game, back to back. I never sat out because I never seemed to tire. I was truly in my element. If I finished the day with torn clothes, a head full of grass, and a few scrapes and bruises, I felt like it was my birthday. When the day ended, I dashed the short distance home, sweat-drenched and hungry, smiling ear to ear, satisfied at the work I had put in for the team. That was my testing ground, and game after game, I passed the test with flying colors.

As fate would have it, I never played a down for VP, but I earned the respect of the boys in my neighborhood every weekend on that little stretch of grass. I did it without pads or a number on my back, and without the OJ Simpson cleats. The chip on my shoulder was all I needed as motivation. At that time, I didn't know that that mindset, a determination to succeed regardless of my stature or ranking, would later take me to places beyond my wildest dreams. I was just happy to be a member of the makeshift team. My mother didn't have a clue.

In sports, as with life, there are underdogs, and there are favorites. In some ways, my life was cast as an underdog from the very beginning. My ability to adapt to my circumstances prepared me to succeed on a larger stage even as an underdog. Outside of winning the Outstanding Defensive Back award my senior year in high school, I was nobody in the world of prep sports. Not even so much as a local newspaper clipping to my name. So the fact that, without fully adjusting to the academic pressures, I decided to try out for the football team at Cal was a huge leap of faith. Truthfully, taking that leap started as a dare of sorts. My dorm buddies, Mel and T-Mac, encouraged me in the way a cat would trap a mouse with a tempting piece of cheese. We were chilling in the dining hall when Mel asked the question. "You started both ways in high school, didn't you?"

His question kind of ignited my process of self-evaluation, almost immediately. Despite being a three-sport athlete and earning seven varsity letters during three years of high school, the thought of playing ball for Cal had never occurred to me.

"You should try walking onto the team. Who knows, you might make it," T-Mac said.

For all I know, Mel and T-Mac exchanged secret grins behind my back, believing I didn't have the heart to try out for the team. But I liked my slim-to-none chances and took the bait.

Most high school athletes that play sports at a major Division I university are recruited and given an athletic scholarship. A financial-aid recipient, I was taking remedial English, remedial math, remedial chemistry, and philosophy. Trying to keep my head above water was my main priority. To make ends meet, I had to work a part-time job washing dishes. And I was going to try out for Cal's football team? What was I thinking? The stats were clear: barely 5 percent of high school students were good enough to play any sport at the collegiate level. I was trying to beat the odds. To entertain such an audacious challenge meant competing with athletes from schools three times the size of my small high school. There would only be a small number of walk-ons to make the team. I was hell-bent on being one of them. Beyond my above-average athletic abilities, I was used to playing at a level bigger than my body. That was one trait that neither genetics nor training could give. But to survive college tryouts, I had to make my body bigger, because this wasn't G Street.

WANNABE

I spent the entire first semester of freshman year training. Attending lectures during the day and working out after my classes sapped my energy like working a push mower in hundred-degree sun. There was little time left for distractions. If it didn't involve running bleachers, lifting weights, or eating, I couldn't be bothered. I did a lot of eating. At one point, I was eating up to five meals a day and drinking protein power shakes mornings and at bedtime.

They say that a watched pot never boils. Well, the same can be said about gaining weight. It was impractical for me to step onto the scale every morning. But I did, looking for a pound of weight gain, some proof positive that I was moving closer to my goal. Eventually, I restrained myself to weekly weigh-ins, although that didn't deter me from my daily inspections in the mirror. Gaining weight proved to be just as hard as losing it during my days on the wrestling team. Either way, trying to cheat your genetics and metabolism is a monster. Eventually, I gained almost ten pounds over the course of five months.

During my physical metamorphosis, I attended home games on Saturdays at Memorial Stadium, a grand coliseum with seating for more than 65,000. My team thundered out of the tunnel and onto the field to my round-eyed amazement. As a mere cheerleader along with thousands of other students, my pulse quickened. Being suited out, running onto the field with my chinstrap buckled, and representing my team as a gladiator in this sport of men was all that I could imagine for my future. *One day, LaMar. One day that will be you out there,* I'd tell myself.

As the weeks went by, the number of wannabes I encountered while working out dwindled. Before long, it was just one other guy and me training together. But there were undoubtedly other wannabes with the dream to play Cal football that I never saw, perhaps training at other times, in other locations. It wasn't easy holding a stopwatch in one hand while sprinting at top speed across the rain-drenched Astroturf, but that's what I did. As if running down a dream, I clocked my sprint times while imagining the sounds of coaches yelling out instructions, whistles sharply blowing. Sometimes I'd even imagine the roar of the crowd. It was a game of make believe that I played with myself. Working out in a stadium so huge made me feel like a tiny man on a larger-than-life mission. It is impossible to capture in words what can only be truly appreciated by those who embark on this journey of sacrifice.

By the time spring ball rolled around, I was training alone. But just as I suspected, there were others who surfaced for tryouts. Many other un-recruited jocks had my dream of playing for the Golden Bears. I didn't know their stories; they didn't know mine. Maybe they played on a surface that was even worse than the sprinkler-riddled patch of grass that I played on near G Street. Perhaps they played on hardened dirt-filled lots scattered with broken glass and debris, and they had scars to prove it. Maybe they could play bigger than their bodies too. There was no way of knowing.

MISFIT

It seemed like every step of my journey was a revealing look behind the scenes of big-time college football. As a potential team member, I was able to walk down corridors that fans were never allowed to see. It was so much more than I could've ever expected. The locker room located inside Memorial Stadium was a fully carpeted space with three-feet-wide wood laminate lockers with shiny brass hooks and combination-locked cubbies.

The main rows of lockers were organized by jersey numbers, grouping players of similar positions in various areas. My locker assignment was not located among those, however. There was another section of the locker room situated off to the side, between the equipment managers' space and the showers. The numbering system for these lockers was different. They were random, redundant numbers with the letter A next to them. My locker was located in this area. Some players in this section were even required to share lockers.

Similar to those banded to the Island of Misfit Toys in one of those Christmas cartoon specials, players located in the wannabe section of the locker room were deemed unworthy, if unproven. We were not even good enough to have a jersey number of our own. Obviously, the numbering system was from one to ninety-nine. There were nearly 120 athletes when spring camp began. About ninety-five made the squad, eighty received scholarships, and only sixty or so traveled to away games. The law of attrition determined who would stay and who would be cut.

My locker assignment was 25-A. Our dark blue helmets had one-inch gold numbers on the back. My number was 25-dot. The dot symbolized the redundant number, or the letter A. The real, legitimate number twenty-five was a senior fullback who traveled to away games and played. I was trying to make the practice roster made up of redshirt freshmen, walk-ons, and third-string players. Called the scout team, this squad had the important assignment of acting as the opposing team. Every week the scout team mimicked another school's plays and schemes, serving almost as live hitting dummies. If the offense had to run the plays repeatedly, we had to absorb the hits repeatedly. I was a redundant alphanumeric player wearing someone else's number. But hey, I was a part of the tryouts. No complaints from me. My last name was on the back of my practice jersey, so I suppose I did have an identity, albeit an obscure one.

Practice lasted about three hours each weekday. I made it to the stadium by two o'clock in the afternoon, undressed, and reported to the training room to get taped. I sat high atop a padded table listening to country music blaring out of the overhead speaker system, making small talk with the athletic trainers, feeling like I was somebody. An undersized kid from G Street, there I was being taped up by a team of professional trainers. Looking to my left and right, I saw scholarship athletes, some future NFL Pro Bowl players, receiving identical treatment. As far as I could tell, I was valued the same. Protecting me from injury was no less of a priority, or so I reasoned.

Outside of my classes, my entire spring semester was devoted to conditioning, weightlifting, Saturday scrimmages, and Sunday film sessions during which we reviewed film from the scrimmages. Every play that took place on the field was graded. If I broke up or intercepted a pass, I'd receive a plus. Hustling and making a tackle earned me a plus grade. If I took an improper angle in pursuit of a ball carrier or missed a tackle, I received minuses. I was given a total percentage for my overall performance.

After surviving three months of spring practices, all I could do wait. I took little comfort in the fact that I intercepted the ball on the last play of the final scrimmage. My first year at Cal ended, and I headed home to San Diego for the summer not knowing my fate. Not everyone knew that I was on edge because I didn't tell many people what I was attempting to do. My family knew. But I was never one for announcing my business or bragging. Working out with my stepdad and going to the gym with my boy Reggie was how I passed the time. Reggie was built like a tank. A red brother with a strong chin and sandy-brown Afro, he seemed to have two passions in life: women and fitness, in that order.

GOLDEN TICKET

It was a long, tense, wait. The summer seemed endless. In between chasing the cuties with Reggie, hitting the gym, working on my footwork with my stepdad, and eating, the days melted away at a snail's pace. I wasn't sure if I would make the cut, but I stayed positive. No matter what, I thought, I needed to be ready just in case. Every protein shake was ingested with that in mind. Nearly six weeks into summer, it came. Dated July 24, 1984, typed on official blue and gold university letterhead and signed by the head football coach, my formal invitation to report to fall camp arrived at my parents' house. It read:

> Dear Lamar,
>
> This is your official invitation to report to Fall Camp on August 14 at the Durant Hotel between 1 pm and 5 pm. This will be the Bears' 102nd season of football. In our last two seasons, we have won 12 games, tied 1,

and lost 9. Four of the wins, and one tie, came in the last minute of play. It's the fourth quarter that counts!

Be ready and hungry to make this year the most important in your football career. 21 days to report, 46 days to Tucson, and 161 days to a January 1 Rose Bowl victory.

Salud!

While I'll admit that Joe Kapp's letter was a bit grandiose for an eighteen-year-old college freshman and wannabe desperate to make the team, it was awe-inspiring. *You did it. You did it!* I repeated that phrase silently as I read my letter over and over again, sitting on the edge of my bed at my parents' house. Mission accomplished. So overjoyed, I felt like Charlie tearing open a Wonka bar and finding the last golden ticket. My dream to play college football was like Charlie's dream to tour Wonka's chocolate factory, and I knew that it would be just as glorious an adventure. With Coach Kapp's golden letter, I was on the team. That was big time for me, huge. All that remained was a nagging question: could I live up to the expectations of the players on my team? Time would tell.

11 | Two-Faced

Girls, parties, cash, personal tours of the campus and athletic facilities and a whole bunch of promises awaited elite athletes during their recruiting trips. For blue-chip athletes, the sky is the limit. But that kind of star treatment only lasts for a short while. When a player commits to a particular school by signing a letter of intent, the honeymoon phase ends quickly. From that point forward, it's less about the hype and all about performance and growth within the system.

Neither blue chip nor someone invited to try out for the team, I was a self-selected wannabe who walked on to prove a point to myself and to experience firsthand big-time college football. The VIP treatment was never wasted on me. The only chip I had was the one on my shoulder I'd been carrying since my G Street glory days. I looked at scholarship athletes with both envy and disdain. Even so, I tried my best to emulate their work ethic, eating habits, training dedication, and swagger. Insecure about my athletic accomplishments, I studied them and tried to fit into the esteemed culture of the elite athletes. I was reaching. Before long, it became apparent that despite their impressive high school accomplishments, some athletes never lived up to expectations on the next level. Because no one had any expectations of me to begin with, I could either sink or swim, and nobody would care in the least. But I was determined to swim.

MORE WITH LESS

After making the team, I was forced to do double duty. Not only did I have to manage football practice, but I also had my studies and the expectations of professors to manage. Both were equally challenging: trying to prove myself as an athlete and trying to prove that I could someday, four or five years down the road, earn a Berkeley degree. The professors who were sports fans—the ones who went to every home game—were supportive, even flexible. They allowed athletes to make up work, do-over failed exams, and other allowances. I've never known a professor to illegally give a passing grade to an athlete that didn't do the work or show up to class, but grade inflation was common.

Then there were the haters, those professors that seemed to resent athletes. They seemed to detest the fact that athletes received privileges of any type, including preferential class scheduling and free books. To me, it was the same disdain that some educators showed toward minority students. Black or brown students gained entry into Cal because of affirmative action, so they thought. So what about athletes? Well, the sentiment was that they were dumb jocks that gained entry into Cal only because of their ability to run or throw a ball. They didn't earn admission based on their intellectual abilities or potential. In reality, I learned that neither stereotype held true. Still, not wanting to be unfairly targeted, I didn't advertise the fact that I was an athlete. For example, I rarely wore my football jersey to classes on Fridays before game day, as was the tradition. Because I didn't wear my identity as an athlete on my sleeve, and because I wasn't a big guy, I flew right under the radar for most professors.

After making the football team, I received help with the time-consuming registration process. Back in the mid-1980s students had to stand in line and sometimes wait for hours on end to get a class they wanted. Athletes didn't wait in long lines. To help ensure that athletes didn't squander their opportunity for a college education, the NCAA progress rules required all athletes to declare a major course of study by the completion of their second year. This rule helped keep me on track, somewhat. I took the minimum of twelve credits per semester, rather than the standard fifteen. It was known as the five-year plan, and most athletes were on that plan. It was rare for an athlete to graduate in four years, even at Berkeley.

Had I passed all of my courses every semester, I would have earned the required 120 credits for graduation in ten semesters, or five years. The downside to my strategy was that I had no margin for error. Failing a class—any class—meant I was immediately ineligible to play ball because I had no buffer to help me meet the twelve-credit minimum required to remain eligible.

HELP WANTED

Study table was another resource for athletes. These tutorial services were made available for all athletes regardless of whether or not you were on scholarship. If you were on a team, any team, you could use the services. It was mandatory that scholarship athletes attend these sessions, but for walk-ons like me, it was optional. There were tutors provided for major subjects like history, English, math, and political science. But even more important than the group tutorials themselves was the atmosphere.

Dinner was served at the study table. Steaks, baked potatoes, salad, corn on the cob, and all the extras. My plate was full every weeknight. It was almost a sign of manhood to pile your plate as high as possible and then grab three glasses of milk. I mean, who drinks three glasses of milk during one meal? Everything was a competition. The amount of food wasted was a crime. Still, we'd try to out-eat each other. To break bread with other fatigued athletes, clown one another, swap war stories, and then settle down to study had a replenishing, unifying effect. Hundreds of athletes, men and women, sat side by side in the Student Union Building studying. It was a room full of jocks from all sports teams bent over books for hours. It was as serious as Sunday school. And I had a seat in the church. It was a place where every congregate was equal in the eyes of the NCAA despite their star qualities on the playing field, or court, or pool, or wherever they competed. For me, those quiet nights reminded me that we were not simply athletes. Like it or not, as student-athletes, we all had two faces.

There were few black professors on campus. My most significant encounter with one took me almost by surprise while I was sitting in one of the larger lecture halls on campus, the Physical Science Lecture Hall in the Pimentel building. It seated about five hundred students and was used mostly for chemistry and physics courses. As usual, I was but one of a handful of dark specks in an audience filled primarily with white and Asian faces. On that particular day, I decided to sit toward the front. As the stage rotated, I looked up to see a sight that amazed and surprised me. It was a black professor. He wore a tweed sports jacket and tie, and he sported a neat Afro. He was frantically scribbling chemistry equations on the board. He finished up, quickly called the class to order, and began to teach chemistry.

Similar to when that aspiring dentist substituted in my class at Chollas Elementary, suddenly I felt like I had a place. His teaching was no different from any other professor that I had up to that point. But his presence resonated in a way that I cannot describe in words. It was like I was proud to be enrolled in that course and proud that he was teaching such a complicated subject to me and hundreds of other students. Professor Lester and I met on only one occasion. I missed a midterm exam and met with him to discuss taking the makeup. He was attentive, thoughtful, and fair. I sat near the front for every lecture I attended. Because of the man that stood in front of me teaching chemistry, I felt especially relevant. That translated into the confidence I needed to pass his class the first time around.

My encounter with another African American professor was altogether different. He was dismissive and treated me with the assumption that I was trying to get over. It was as if he wanted me to know that his Afro-American Studies course was no cakewalk. It was no easy A. Perhaps struggling with his inferiority complex, he assumed the role of anti-mentor, someone who held the holy grail of letters and would be damned if he was going to hand them over to any black person that walked through Sather Gate. *What would I look like walking into that course and that man's psychology?* Sensing trouble and knowing better, I elected to drop his course.

There was another professor that had a profound impact on me even though, ironically, I never enrolled in any of his classes. Nor did I meet him the entire time that I spent at Berkeley. His name was Dr. Harry Edwards. A six-foot-eight, 300-pound black man with a glistening bald head and full goatee, he wore dark shades like brothers back in the Black Power days. The only thing more intimidating than his physical stature was the blunt truth he espoused according to his analysis. Subconsciously, I was worried about what his class would teach me and where his advice might lead me as a fledgling student and newbie collegiate athlete. A former collegiate athlete who had opted out of the NFL draft, Dr. Edwards was the preeminent expert on the sociology of sport. He was the architect of the Olympic Project for Human Rights, which led to the Black Power Salute protest, including the raised black fists in the air by African American athletes at the 1968 Summer Olympics in Mexico City.

Dr. Edwards made powerful observations about athletes, in particular black athletes, and how sports mirrored the problems found in the larger society, including racism, drugs, and corruption. He preached responsibility and encouraged black athletes to hitch their futures to academic pursuits rather than sports achievements, even if their athletic talents paved the way for a college education. Instinctively, I knew what Dr. Edwards would say about my dilemma about whether or not to continue to play football. All black athletes who paid attention knew his opinion even if we could never hear the gospel truth directly from the professor. Strategically, his classes were scheduled for late afternoon, a time when athletes were required to attend sports practice. It was widely known that this was by design.

One of the few safe havens for me at Berkeley was the Student Support Services housed in wooden bungalows called the T-buildings. The buildings didn't look like much from the outside. In fact, they looked more like farm housing than a center for academic support. But those drafty structures offered basic tutorial services—usually led by brilliant instructors that looked like hippies—for most of the core subjects. But the quality of the reviews varied considerably.

BOB THE BUILDER

Another place to go for assistance and mentorship was the Professional Development Program (PDP). The PDP was a workshop-style tutorial to assist minority students in math and science. Top-shelf graduate-student instructors were committed to supporting lost students like me. And every tutor was hand-selected by a man that would later become one of my long-time mentors, Dr. Bob Fullilove.

Bob was distinguished in his understated, laid-back demeanor and personal style. He never said it aloud, but based on his approach, his motto for higher learning must have been "This shit is not all that hard if you apply yourself and get a little help."

An educator, Bob had a genuine passion for teaching beyond the classroom. He carried the rank of assistant professor at the most prestigious public university in the nation. To look at him, you would never know it. A coffee-colored black man with a short Afro, he wore un-ironed khaki pants, the occasional knit tie, sneakers, and earrings in both ears. Bob spoke in a down-home vernacular when he wasn't speaking in French. The epitome of a modern-day renaissance man, he was somewhat unconventional by some university standards, insisting that everyone call him Bob and not professor or doctor. But when you talked to him, even in the most casual conversation, his swagger, quick smile, immense knowledge, and spot-on advice about academics, survival, and life revealed his real genius.

Bob coached hundreds of students through the obstacles of college life. He helped students plot a course to graduate school, reviewed their applications, wrote letters of recommendation, and assisted them with designing a contingency plan. Bob was the truth, the real deal. A teacher in the broadest sense, Bob was deeply rooted in self-improvement and uplifting the community. He led a purpose-driven academic life. Thus, he stood in the gap for countless minority students. Truth be told, his towering presence, the PDP, and a handful of other supporters made my survival on a predominantly white university campus possible.

12 | Hidden Agenda

The best players don't always start, or even play for that matter. I learned that from my stepdad.

"Coaches sometimes go with the player that is more consistent, not always the best athlete," my stepdad, a college standout and eleven-year NFL veteran, told me. "Then there are the politics, the likeability factors, and, of course, luck. It all plays a role."

My stepdad and I spent countless hours working out during the summers when I came home from Berkeley. We ran hundreds of flights of stairs leading from the overflow parking area at San Diego State University. We worked on improving my backward running, or backpedaling, on the field. Along the way, he gave me many pointers on playing the position of defensive back. He also laid some knowledge on me about sports psychology. That pearl about coaches not always playing the most talented players stuck with me. Time and again, I saw for myself how it played out. Experience taught me that while some people are born with great athletic ability and physical attributes, it's the combination of talent, attitude, and opportunity that determines one's success in a sport. Opportunities are often politically determined.

To my surprise, I witnessed superior players passed over because of their poor attitudes. Usually, scholarship athletes got the nod over equally qualified walk-ons, presumably because the financial investment was there. But in rare cases, the reverse happened:

walk-ons with average skill but good attitudes, game smarts, and a great work ethic started over paid players. Darryl, a friend of mine, was the poster child for what a walk-on athlete could achieve. After spending his redshirt year on the practice squad, he ended up starting at strong safety for four years. Even so, the notion of an even playing field was anything but even.

Sure, all the players are given the same rules to follow. But the rules could be flexed depending on who you were, on and off the field. I learned that reality firsthand when I missed curfew during spring ball. My good friend Dexter, another walk-on DB, and I were on our way back from a team dinner at the faculty club. We were returning to the Durant Hotel, our home during training camp, when we were distracted by two young women hanging out the window flirting with us. We had our marching orders, the same as the other players on the team, but the temptation was too great to resist.

We sneaked out of the hotel, scooped up the girls, and walked the campus looking for a spot to make out with our dates. We slipped back into our rooms later that night and missed our 10:00 p.m. bed check. We braced ourselves for the consequences the next day. Coach gave no indication that we were in trouble during the entire practice. We finished our wind sprints with the team and then took off our helmets and shoulder pads and headed toward the tunnel leading to the locker room with everyone else.

"Hazzi and Jonesy, I need to see you," Coach said.

Here it comes, I thought.

"Go ahead and sit your pads down," Coach continued. "You both owe me for missing curfew last night." He pointed to the bleachers.

Busted. It was wishful thinking to hope for better.

"How many do we have to do?" I asked.

"Just start running. I'll tell you when to stop," Coach replied.

Dexter and I looked at each other with dread and started our long climb up the A-section of the stadium near the north tunnel. About eighty rows steep, we ran to the top fifteen times before our punishment ended. I was not only exhausted; I was pissed off. All I could focus on was my trip to the showers and putting an end to a miserable day, but Coach had another idea. He wanted to give us a lecture. Because I wasn't trying to hear all of that, I tuned him out.

On another occasion, however, I was all ears. During a losing streak, Coach gathered all of the defensive backs together for an odd type of pep talk.

"Listen. You guys need to realize that you're playing against guys from Arizona, Oregon State, and Washington State. Some of these guys are in school just to play football. They're not there for an education. You guys need to get your priorities straight," Coach reasoned.

My teammates and I looked at one another. Of course, no one said a thing, but if they felt like me, they were all mortified.

Coach Bob Dipipi, our DB coach, continued, "You need to stop spending so much time in those school books and spend more time learning your playbook."

Yeah, but we ain't at Oregon State, I thought. *We at Berkeley. And I is here to get my edumacation, Massa.* I might have looked like a slave, and, true, I was playing for free, but I was nobody's fool. My priority was to get my degree. Everything else was gravy. Even in my exhausted state, I knew that Coach was full of hot air. We all knew that. Coach was apparently worried about his own longevity. Playing well improved the team's chances of winning. The more wins the team amassed, the more job protection he had. It was all about his self-preservation. Coach apparently cared more about his future than ours. They say there's no interest like self-interest.

College sports, especially football, generate lots of money. It's big-time business to the tune of hundreds of millions of dollars. There are television rights, corporate sponsorships, and stadium expansions, not to mention ticket and merchandise sales. Football programs use that cash to improve facilities, gaining a competitive edge in recruiting, providing a greater opportunity to appear in a bowl game and job security for the coaching staff. I get that now. And given the potential revenue, combined with pressures of job security, it's not surprising that coaches, athletic directors, boosters, and other university officials cut corners and promote hidden agendas. Before that talk with my position coach, I never even considered that coaches might have ulterior motives. Naïve, I always figured that coaches coached because of their love for the game or their commitment to helping shape boys into men, teaching them lessons along the way and equipping them with skills for life.

Football can be viewed as an analogy for life. That's what I was told since I was a little boy, and I drank the Kool-Aid, probably because I heard it so many times. Players learn life lessons by struggling through adversity, putting on their game face, never quitting. Sports can also be a means to an end, a vehicle to get a college education. Those were comparisons that I heard throughout my entire athletic career. Sometimes it held true, sometimes not.

At Cal, my team had its share of players who would have never had a shot in hell to obtain a Berkeley degree except for through their athletic talents. As unprepared as I was for college work, there were others from schools around the country, down south in particular, where it seemed that reading was not fundamental. Sadly, when it came to schoolwork, some of my teammates were struggling. Several teammates, it seemed, were more coachable on the field than in the classroom. It became apparent to me that some coaches could care less beyond keeping them eligible to play ball. Years after my playing days were over, I had an experience that confirmed this peculiar value system.

"So where are you thinking about going?" my friend asked. The young man mentioned a college but not the one where he coached.

"Really?" my friend replied. "You're not considering playing for me?"

The kid, who was holding a football when we encountered him, began to toss the ball up in the air, alternating it between his right and left hands. He was a good-sized kid and looked athletic enough. It was the typical scenario that you might expect: low-income apartment complex, several children, a single mother, and no father in the home. It was a story that I knew only too well.

The kid hesitated and then responded, "I don't know. I think I might want to play for A&M." He was referring to a Division

I-AA program in the Southwestern Athletic Conference located in Alabama.

"How do your grades look?" my friend asked.

Embarrassed, the young man replied, "Not good. I'm failing two subjects right now."

"Well I can tell you right now, you're not going to be able to play at A&M with those grades. But if you come and play for me, we can get you on the field, maybe even next year," said my friend.

The kid lit up like a Christmas tree. There was no discussion about getting a degree or NCAA academic progress requirements for that matter. No talk about the academic support services or possible areas that the young man might choose to study, albeit that might have been implied. There was only the half-baked promise, if you could even call it that, of getting onto the field and playing ball.

I happened to witness the encounter by chance. At the invitation of a close friend, I was in Alabama for a Football Classic, a competition traditionally held between two HBCU teams. While running errands with my friend, an assistant head coach at a local university, I happened upon the young man's home for an informal recruiting pitch. Of course, I had no earthly idea how the kid would be eligible to enroll in school, let alone play ball, with two failing grades. That was disturbing enough. But what astounded me most about the exchange was the message that was being sent to that kid. I was surprised that someone who had graduated college would appear so single-minded. But there again, I was reminded of the principle of self-preservation.

13 | Failure to Launch

It was a routine Saturday scrimmage, another opportunity for me to showcase my skills. Cameras were always rolling from the skybox. And that's when it happened. It was another example of an athlete giving up the ghost. My former dorm mate and friend took a hand-off, broke the line of scrimmage, and was gaining positive yardage. Just as he was making his way into the secondary, *bam!* A collision that sounded like a car crash stopped him dead in his tracks. Alex, the backup strong safety, hit him helmet-to-helmet on the dead run and knocked my friend two or three yards in the opposite direction. Man down! The only movement seen was the ball slowly rolling out of his unclenched arm.

The hit heard 'round the stadium was symbolic. The impact of the blow altered more than his running path. It seemed to alter his trajectory as an athlete. It was as if the ghost of that much sought-after, highly recruited athlete from a 5A high school in Texas got up off of the AstroTurf and floated out of him toward sports heaven. My dazed friend was helped to his feet by the team trainers who walked him to the bench for a respite. That hit and the likely concussion that it caused seemed to knock the confidence out of him. His swagger was dampened, and his play from that point forward was tentative. Like a vicious cycle, the decline of his confidence appeared to lead to a gradual decline in his playing time.

BODY AND MIND

An athlete suffering from poor sports psychology will undermine himself. If you can't get your mind right, you can't get your game right. Nobody tells you that. You're just expected to manage. I got caught up many times. When I witnessed that happen to my friend, I reflected on an experience I had while still in high school. It was my senior year, and I couldn't catch the ball to save my life. You wouldn't think that something I had done since the age of five would leave my muscle memory. But when suffering from low sports esteem, even the simplest tasks are fleeting. For a span of about two weeks, I couldn't catch a cold. Every time the ball traveled toward me, I panicked. I had a big case of performance anxiety. I dropped the ball mentally even before it was within my physical grasp. It got so bad that I wished that Rudy, my high school quarterback, wouldn't throw it to me.

I had to tackle my fear of failure, and I knew it. Eventually, Rudy and I stayed after practice and worked it out through a simple game of catch. After every practice, we would play catch for up to thirty minutes. No pressure, no competition. It was just two friends tossing the ball back and forth. I caught a few passes out of the backfield in the following game. Then, during a Friday night game, I snapped the mental funk with one play. I caught a leaping pass over a defender along the sideline that was good for a forty-yard gain and set up a score.

Assuming an athlete can weather the psychological threats to success, there are two other potential pitfalls to navigate: physical injury and academic setbacks. Physical injury always looms large in full-contact sports like football. In college, I witnessed blue-chip athletes get hurt during their redshirt freshman year. One hit, and boom, just like that, their career ended without a single play experienced in a real game. Knees, ankles, hamstrings, and collarbones were all common points of injury. For me, the wear and tear showed up on my left shoulder. It began to dislodge chronically. This injury required the trainers to pop it back into the socket. What was writhing pain instantaneously was relieved with one fast tug on my shoulder. Dealing with my personal limitations was one thing. But seeing some of my teammates face even more terrible injuries gave me cause to pause. If a blue-chipper could get injured, then no one was immune, not even a kid with an oversized heart from G Street.

All of the ball players got dinged up on a regular basis. That was expected. When it happened, we relied on a team of trainers to fix us up. The team was led by a good old country boy named Bob. From ice buckets to moist heating pads and everything in between, Bob and his team of country-music-loving trainers managed to patch up my teammates and me. At a second's notice, Bob would run onto the field and pull out a pair of tape-cutting scissors, a roll of tape, a bag of ice, or call for a stretcher. The only thing quicker than Bob's response to an injured player was his razor-sharp wit. He was a legend for the stories he'd tell to incoming rookies. No story was more famed than the one about the bulls:

Two young bulls are standing on the top of a hill, looking down at a pasture full of cows, when one young bull turns to the other and says, "My, my, don't those cows look good? I have a right mind to run down there and screw one of them." The older bull hears them, shakes his head, and says, "See, that's the problem with you young bulls. You're so green behind the ears that you don't know any better. You stand here looking at all that fine tail, and you want to run down there and screw one of them. I say we walk down there ... and screw 'em all!"

It was a riot. Every year during a team meal, with his thick southern draw, Bob would take center stage and tell that particular story. After which Bob introduced his team of trainers and gave a speech about the importance of preventing injuries during training camp and the regular season. His main target was the rookies, or young bulls, who didn't know enough to know that they didn't know much of anything.

MAKING THE GRADE

Bob and his crew couldn't save all of us. But between them and our strength and conditioning work, most of us got through the season in one piece. My shoulder injury continued to be a problem. However, the bigger problem was my failure to progress academically. During the spring of 1985, I failed second-semester calculus for the second time. I don't know what made me think that I could take calculus in a self-paced format. It required the kind of discipline I did not have. Attending reviews, meeting with the tutors, and keeping up with my lessons was not a part of my game plan. Instead, I blew it off the same way I blew off my laundry: I didn't do wash until *everything* was dirty.

My comeback plan going into the summer was to take a class at a local community college in San Diego and transfer the credit. But summer fun-and-sun was calling me after class. I goofed off with my boy Reggie, working out, hanging at the beach, and chasing cuties. Reggie, my partner in most of my capers, didn't have the same priorities that I did. He wasn't in school full-time. He wasn't playing college ball, but he was a hell of a lot of fun.

Against my better judgment, I chose to run with the wolves that summer. Spending nights out on double dates and moonlit picnics with my latest summer fling did little to advance my studies. Instead of wading through the pages of my textbooks, I opted to wade through the choppy black waters of the Pacific Ocean at South Mission Beach, skinny-dipping late night. My priorities were all screwed up. Eventually, my attendance in class ceased altogether.

When I returned to Cal in the fall, I learned the grim news: I was ineligible to play football. The news was paralyzing. My mouth was dry and my stomach churned as I staggered to the locker room to ponder my reality. Having only a vague understanding of the NCAA progress rules, I had thrown away my chance to break into the lineup and travel to away games. *So much for having no academic buffer.* As a result, the entire year as a varsity athlete was lost, and I felt lost along with it. I failed to launch my athletic career. Losing my uphill battle, I began to wonder if I'd remain a self-selected wannabe. I spent the season on the practice squad and then underwent surgery to fix my shoulder. The ball-in-socket joint was corrected by placing a screw in my shoulder. Months of rehab during the off-season and a shoulder brace allowed me to continue competing on the field.

TRIPPED UP

My first start at the cornerback position should have come against Boston College the following year. Our starting right cornerback, Sidney, was injured. That opened another window of opportunity. I was healthy, able, and willing. But I had tripped myself up yet again. The ad that appeared in the *Daily Californian*, Berkeley's campus newspaper, read, "Get your 1986 Men of Moods II Calendar now! Featuring some of Cal's hottest athletes." The picture in the ad was of yours truly. The project was the brainchild of an entrepreneur and photographer affectionately known by many as Uncle Nate.

Nate was a nerdy-looking street professor who had to be in his midforties at the time. He stood about five six with rounded shoulders and glasses, and he had an infectious sense of humor. He had an opinion about everything and everybody, usually backward and prejudiced. He somehow had it in his head that he could make a ton of money with this beefcake calendar that he named Moods. He would often walk the campus with his camera bag over his shoulder as if he was on official business. Eventually, he would befriend athletes, recruiting them for his project. I was one of twelve black male athletes, including three other football players, approached to be featured in his calendar. I had no idea that I was breaking any rules. Hell, I only made one hundred dollars for the shoot. The small payment and fifteen minutes of fame were hardly worth the punishment.

The news of my NCAA infraction came by formal letter. The letter stated,

"Your photograph is displayed in the 1986 Men of Moods II calendar. Your involvement with the calendar is a violation of NCAA Constitution Article C3-1-(e), which prohibits the use of a student-athlete's picture on any commercial item."

In the big scheme of things, it was a minor infraction to be sure. I wasn't a star (or even a recognizable) athlete, and I sure was not receiving royalties for my appearance in the calendar. Depressed that I couldn't win for losing, it didn't seem like I would ever get onto the field. That was a time when I wished that I had a real counselor or advisor, someone to watch my back the way they would look after the scholarship athletes. Instead, I was guiding myself, and to my peril. For me, it was trial and error. I confronted trial after trial, and I seemed to make error after error.

After giving back the measly amount of money, I appealed my case in person to the NCAA. My penalty was reduced, but it still cost me a one-game suspension. Another huge opportunity was spent. We lost that game by a score of 15–21. If the first setback did not convince me, this penalty did. For the first time, I understood that the NCAA rules and regulations were no joke. From that point forward, I pledged to follow the rules. After all of the stops and stutters, I finally made my Division-I debut the following week. We beat Washington State 31–21 at home. My athletic college football career had launched, but unfortunately, our team was crashing and burning.

The win against Washington State would be the only one for eight straight weeks. The PAC-10 was packed with nationally ranked teams that year. Outgunned, we got our behinds chewed up by a schedule of opponents that included twelfth-ranked Washington, nineteenth-ranked UCLA, fourteenth-ranked Arizona, fifth-ranked Arizona State, and thirteenth-ranked USC. It was brutal.

As it turned out, my coach's concerns for his longevity were well founded. After the second consecutive losing season, a coaching change was made. Following our embarrassing 50–18 loss against Washington University, Coach Joe Kapp expressed his frustration by unzipping his pants in front of the Seattle media. Following that stunt, he was notified that he would be terminated after the 1986 Big Game, played at Berkeley.

Entering the game with a 1–9 record, we were twenty-one-point underdogs against Stanford. But we were the better team on that Saturday. We pulled off one of the greatest Big Game upsets that year.

Responding to the student section's pregame chants of "Win one for the zipper," we beat the number-sixteen, nationally ranked and Gator-Bowl-bound Stanford Cardinals 17–11. We carried Coach Kapp out of the stadium amid pandemonium, with the student section chanting "We want Kapp! We want Kapp!" Despite the wishes of the student section, Coach Kapp wasn't coming back. Legendary player and head coach Joe Kapp was fired, along with most of his staff, including my coach, Coach Bob Dipipi.

With a change of the guard came a change of attitude. It looked like my return to the team was in jeopardy. This time, it wasn't because of being tripped up by eligibility rules. Having finally launched as a player, I was growing tired of being exploited. It was time to be compensated.

14 | Getting Paid

While growing up, the easiest way to get money was to collect bottles and cans and return them to a store for the deposit. The problem was that all the other kids in my neighborhood searched the same empty lots and trash cans that I did. Therefore, it wasn't very reliable. Pickings were slim. Washing cars was a better gig. My friends and I would join forces and become a mobile car-washing service. We brought the business right to the customer, walking the entire neighborhood with a bucket, a small bottle of liquid soap, and a few rags. We might even have a bottle of Windex and a stack of newspapers for cleaning windows.

I was assertive when it came to making money. I'd go door-to-door and be the first to speak up. "Hi. Would you like to have your car washed today?"

Most people would refuse, but now and then someone would agree. Our going rate was one dollar a car—a bargain for them and a good little profit for us. One car would pay for our soap. The rest was profit. But by far, the best hustle to have on G Street was working for Mr. Dixon selling peanut brittle for the Sickle Cell Anemia Association.

Mr. Dixon was a short, stocky, yellow brother with a large, curly Afro and a forked tongue. He was shady at best and downright crooked at worst. If his mouth was moving, he was working some angle.

"I want everyone to take a cotton ball and wet it with rubbing alcohol. Now, wipe the back of your neck and take a look at it," Mr. Dixon directed.

I followed his instructions.

"Is it dirty?" he'd ask.

Of course it was.

"If you're going to work for me, you need to be clean and neat," he'd say.

Those demonstrations were all a part of job training. Boys were required to wear a shirt with a collar and tuck their shirts into their slacks. Girls had to wear a dress or skirt and blouse. The kids that worked for Mr. Dixon were poor but neat and presentable.

"Excuse me, ma'am, my name is LaMar. I'm selling peanut brittle to help raise money to fight Sickle Cell Anemia. Would you like to buy a box of peanut brittle or make a donation today?" Occasionally someone would ask about the disease.

"Sickle cell is a rare blood disorder that affects Afro-Americans mostly. It can cause low blood count, tiredness, pain, infections, and a shorter life span," I would respond.

Mr. Dixon drove a pickup truck with a camper cab top. He collected a truckload of neighbor kids and dropped us off at distant malls, high-traffic stores, or middle-class neighborhoods. Working door-to-door was the worst. Toting a big box of individually wrapped smaller boxes of peanut brittle house to house was unsettling. I had no idea if I would run up against a dog, a shotgun, or some redneck homeowner who wanted to chase me off their property. When Mr. Dixon pulled up to the desired location, he'd stop the truck, look back over his right shoulder, and point to one of us.

"Okay, you—you're getting out here," he would say.

I never knew where I would be dropped off ahead of time. Luckily, on most occasions I had my big brother, LaSalle, nearby. Mr. Dixon would drive through strange neighborhoods, and one by one each kid would climb out of the truck with a donation can or a large box full of peanut brittle. Once or twice during the day, Mr. Dixon came to check on us but mostly to replenish our stocks of candy and swap out our full donation cans for empty ones.

G Street Lion

The work was not easy, soliciting all day, but we made good money. Hard work could yield anywhere between twenty-five and eighty bucks every two weeks! That was unheard of legal cash for a teenager in my neighborhood. We got twenty-five cents for every box of candy or dollar we collected. I suspect that Mr. Dixon received more.

My biggest payday from Mr. Dixon may have been forty dollars, but I received nearly twenty times that amount for a single day's work once. My mother had a brief modeling career and along the way did print ads and TV commercials. She signed my brothers and me up with her agent, Tina Real. I was twelve. Right out of the gate, I landed a big ad for Billy the Kid clothing. I was fitted with a casual outfit and paired with a slightly younger white boy. There was little acting involved. All we did was play games while wearing the clothes. The filming took place at Sea World in San Diego. I had my trailer, makeup person, a personal tutor for my school work, and catered breakfast and lunch. I felt like Rodney Allen Rippy, the famous child star that did the Jack in the Box television commercials back in the day.

One week later, I collected a fat check from my agent for about eight hundred dollars! It was a great day. My mom and I drove to the bank to cash my check.

"Can I hold it?" I asked when we left the bank.

My mom smiled at me. "Yes, you can hold it," she said.

Holding eight hundred dollars made me feel like a million bucks. After the ten-minute ride home from the bank, I never again saw my earnings. Later, I booked ads for Peter Paul candy bars and Ford cars. Each time, my earnings were absorbed into the household to keep us afloat. Still, I felt proud to have made a contribution of some magnitude.

PAY TO PLAY

Early on in college, I washed dishes in the dorm dining commons, and later in co-op housing for international students for money. But when I became a student-athlete, I had to give all that up. Because of my hectic schedule, I could only work during the summer. As a football player, I got the hookup and could choose from plenty of great summer jobs. I needed real financial help during the school year. Trying to make it with a combination of financial aid and the occasional care package from my parents, I struggled. It was time for something better to happen.

No longer relegated to the scout squad of hitting dummies, I was getting lots of playing time, competing for a starting cornerback spot, and I was a special teams captain. Because of my success, I entered my last spring training camp, going into my senior year, with a bit of unease. In my opinion, I was contributing to the team in a substantial way. The problem was that I was doing it all for free. This fact was beginning to rub me the wrong way. It bothered me so much that I scheduled a one-on-one sit-down with Coach Kapp before he departed for good.

It wasn't often that a role player like me met individually with the head football coach at a major university. Usually I'd meet with my position coach to discuss my issues, and he'd work it up the chain of command. However, desperate times required desperate measures, and I needed my fifteen minutes of face-to-face time with the lame-duck coach to make my case.

While sitting in the waiting area outside of Coach Kapp's office, I became indignant. During the ten-minute wait, my eyes darted around the room, bouncing off the plush carpet, lavish office furniture, and ornately framed memorabilia. Then my eyes locked onto Jennifer, Coach Kapp's very pretty, very pregnant secretary with his child. *Scandalous!*

There I sat pretending that somehow it was acceptable. I was burning up, thinking how some guys had all the luck. Coach Kapp could lay claim to a 65,000-seat coliseum, a team of one hundred revenue-generating men, a dozen devoted staff, *and* have his pretty secretary to boot. But there I was bound by voluntary servitude, scraping for a few dollars to ease my burden. Nothing about the situation seemed fair to me. Nothing. So my time had come to speak out.

"LaMar, come on in, young man," Coach Kapp said as he cracked his door wide enough to wave his arm at me.

I entered with a big lump in my stomach. As I entered, I gazed at his embarrassment of riches that adorned his office. His massive, glass-covered desk was immaculate. There he sat in his high-back leather chair, swaying softly with a grin that only Joe Kapp could flash. Like most of my teammates, I had never actually seen the inside of Coach's office. The legendary Joe Kapp, dubbed by *Sports Illustrated* as the "toughest Chicano in pro football" and the only player at that time to have played quarterback in the Super Bowl, Rose Bowl, and Canada's Grey Cup, stared at me.

"So how can I help you?" he asked.

"Oh, um, I wanted to talk to you about my financial situation." It was my turn to state my business. His question snapped me out of the trance I was in, fixed on his Rose Bowl memorabilia. Then I methodically argued the merits of my case, elaborating my concerns with playing for free and how I needed athletic aid. I talked, and Coach Kapp listened. In the end, he told me that he might have a few athletic scholarships to spare before he departed. He promised to do what he could for me.

A few weeks after my talk with the head coach, he announced that he was awarding scholarships to our long snapper and another reserve player. Then Coach Kapp vanished like the fading smoke from the blast of the stadium cannon sounding the end of the game at Memorial Coliseum. I was left without a scholarship and little assurance. It was as if my conversation with him had never occurred. I was back to square one.

SECOND PITCH

The new head coach and former Los Angeles Rams assistant, Bruce Snyder, arrived on the scene a few months later. After taking some time to feel him out, I approached him about my situation. Before the end of spring ball, I scheduled a meeting with Coach Snyder. I felt like a salesperson on a cold call.

"What can I do for you?" Coach Snyder asked.

"Well, Coach, I wanted to tell you about a conversation I had with Coach Kapp before he left."

"Go ahead."

"Well, he said that he would put me on scholarship if he could. Now he's gone, and that obviously didn't happen. I wanted to ask if you could look into it."

My new head football coach looked at me like I was trying to hustle him. "I'm sure you know that we only have a limited number of scholarships," he countered.

"Yes, I do," I said. "But I also feel that I am deserving of one. I'm competing for the starting right cornerback spot. I'm special teams captain, and I have a lot of potential."

"You'll be a senior, son. It's a little late for potential. Potential is important as a sophomore," he said flatly.

Scrambling for a comeback, I said, "True. But I'm a contributor right now. And unlike some other players that are contributing less and getting paid, I'm volunteering *and* working part-time. That makes it harder for me."

Coach paused in silence. His expression was more vacant than pensive, which told me that he didn't understand my desperation. Not only was I forced to work part-time to make ends meet, but sometimes getting paid meant driving nearly one hundred miles northwest in my teammate's broken-down Nissan 240Z.

Like the summer Dexter and I drove to a job in Monte Rio, California. It was a camp located on 2,700 acres of redwood forest, a luxury playground for the global elite called the Bohemian Grove. A place known as a destination where the rich and powerful go to misbehave and participate in occult rituals. The Grove is a private, all-male club with an exclusive membership list that has included every Republican US president since 1923, many Democratic presidents, other cabinet officials, world leaders, corporate tycoons, and even select entertainers.

Too naïve to research my place of employment, I was clueless about its occult reputation and reputed affiliation with the skull and bones society or the ritualistic practices or secret meetings. I thought myself privileged to park high-end luxury cars just outside the gates guarded by secret service and local law enforcement, and later packaging groceries at the Grove for the summer. It was a good-paying job set up by the friends of the Big C Society, Cal's well-to-do alumni boosters. No one told us where we were or who was there. Dexter and I had absolutely no clue.

"Which one of you guys is the smartest?" an old man addressed Dexter and me on the first day, as if we were dumb jocks. Speechless, neither of us replied at first.

"Well, I'm the oldest," I said.

Don't ask me why I responded the way I did. A knee-jerk response that makes me ashamed today, I probably felt compelled to give the man an answer, even if it was a dumb one. Turns out our boss was trying to decide which of us to assign the job of keeping store inventory. We made the decision to share the task.

Sitting in Coach's office, impatiently waiting for him to respond positively to my request, I wondered if he felt as my summer boss had felt, that I was a dumb jock who didn't know my worth.

"I tell you what," Coach Snyder finally said. "I'll talk to some of the coaches and get back to you as soon as I can. How's that sound?"

"Sounds fair to me, Coach. I really appreciate it," I said as I looked him in the eyes and firmly shook his hand like a man.

Knowing that I did all that I could do for my case, I left his office. Beaming, I felt real proud for standing up for myself. That pride carried me through my summer workouts. Now with a renewed hope, I had one last thing to prove. It felt kind of like wanting to be taken in the first round of the little-guy draft on G Street. When the decision letter arrived early summer, I just knew that I'd have good news. I secretly took the letter to my room, closed the door, sat on the edge of my bed, and slowly tore the letter open. *This is my moment.* I kept saying that to myself. *It's now or never.* My heart hammered against my chest, swollen from so many repetitions bench-pressing that summer. As I slid the letter out of the envelope, my heart immediately dropped to the pit of my stomach. It wasn't good news at all. The letter read as follows:

> Because of the NCAA regulations regarding initial awards and limitation on total numbers, I am not able to recommend an award for you at this time. Obviously, this is not the news you were looking for. You are a good member of the Cal football squad, and I hope the circumstances do not present too great of a burden.

Needless to say, regardless of the apologetic tone, the verdict fell way short of my expectations. I was passed over by two head coaches in the span of six months. But Brad, the long snapper, got a free ride. The guy's job was to snap the ball to the kicker or punter. He had no other role besides that one. That did not sit right with me and got me to thinking. Was I just supposed to let the coaches treat me like I wasn't worthy of a scholarship? I couldn't live with that. My internal sense of injustice grew into a noticeable chip on my shoulder.

The chip grew bigger every day until, by the time the team traveled to Santa Rosa, California, for summer training camp, it couldn't be ignored. While going through ball drills with the defensive backs, I experienced an overwhelming need to protest; I guess it's what you'd call passive-aggressive behavior. I'd backpedal, break in the direction indicated by coach, and then catch the ball. I was expected to toss the ball back to the coach and get in the back of the line. Instead, I tossed the ball at Coach's feet, forcing him to bend down, and sometimes even run down, and fetch the ball. After a few errant tosses, along with my unapologetic posture, Coach deduced that my behavior was purposeful. During the stretching period at practice the following day, my position coach approached me.

"What's going on with you, Hasbrouck?" Coach Snow asked, sensing that something was distracting me.

"I might not be around for much longer due to financial hardships,"

I answered. It was my way of saying that I was done playing for free. I was over it.

"Let's talk to Coach Snyder after practice," Coach said. He didn't appear all that surprised to hear my response.

ULTIMATUM

So I made my third trip to the office of the head coach to discuss the same matter: an athletic scholarship. This time, my position coach sat next to me. This trip would be my last, no matter what the outcome, I told myself. Pay me or lose me. That would be my ultimatum. There were no two ways about it. I was at peace with my decision and was prepared to walk away from the team and the sport I loved.

The tone of the meeting was very different. It was more serious than before. It was all business. When you are a man willing to lose it all, you have a psychological advantage in negotiations. That is not to say that I wasn't nervous; I was nervous and afraid. Like having to end a long relationship, it was the kind of fear that you get when you're faced with losing that thing that you love the most. Football was like a dear friend to me. The possibility of losing it was something that I hated to think about, but I knew I had to risk what I loved to get what I deserved. Besides, the bitterness I felt about being wronged was beginning to sap the fun out of playing the game I discovered on G Street.

"So what's going on?" Coach Snyder asked, as if he didn't know the deal.

You know damn well what's going on. I've had enough of being exploited. It's my senior year. It's time for you to show me the money. Of course, my actual reply was more diplomatic.

"I told Coach Snow that I may need to walk away from the team if I don't get the financial support that I feel I deserve." I swallowed hard. My palms were sweating. My heart was racing. It was face-the-music time, and I had to stay in character.

Coach Snyder fired back, "You could walk away just like that?"

"I have nothing left to prove. I'm competing for the starting cornerback spot. I'm a captain on special teams. I started out as an un-recruited walk-on and worked my way to becoming a real contributor to the team, and I've been doing it for free this whole time," I said with my back stiffening.

The coaches looked at each other as if they were communicating telekinetically. I couldn't tell you what they were saying, but I can tell you that it didn't derail my line of reasoning.

I continued, "I'm juggling school, practice, and working a part-time job. No one else is doing all that. Yes, I can walk away. I don't want to, but I could. I have nothing left to prove. I'm at peace with it. Yes."

Coach Snyder sighed reflectively. Nodding, he said, "I think we may be able to work something out." The meeting ended.

The following day, I lay with my back against the firm AstroTurf, stretching before practice. With the warm sun on my face, I looked up at the distant sky, pondering my future on the team. Suddenly, a silhouette stood over me, blocking the sun.

"You got your scholarship. Stop by the office after practice," a voice from above me spoke.

Straining, I squinted but could barely make out the face of my position coach, Coach Snow, against my blue sky. Without uttering a word, I nodded firmly, trying my best to stay in character. As soon as he walked away, I let out an audible sigh of relief. It was like a huge weight had been lifted off my shoulders. It was the weight of that chip. For the first time in the three years on the team, I had a book allowance, paid tuition, and room and board. Most importantly, I could continue playing the sport I loved.

I wanted to stand on the top of Strawberry Canyon and scream for joy that I was validated and that my fight was won. But I did no such thing. Instead, I waited for football practice to end so that I could call my parents to let them know the good news. First, I wanted them to know that I hadn't wasted my precious time playing college football. Second, I wanted my folks to know that I was good enough at the sport to earn an athletic scholarship. After all, universities don't pay for any athlete, only those who are above average, extraordinary. That is what I was, after all. And finally, that was how I felt.

The very next day of practice, I bopped onto the field with a whole new attitude. It was amazing what that gesture of affirmation from the coaches did for me. It was similar to the time my previous defensive back coach, Bob Dipippi, told me that I could cover the wide receivers one-on-one at my discretion. It meant that he had confidence in my skills and judgment. I rose to the occasion then, and I planned to do the same with this opportunity.

Validated. Finally, I was determined to show anyone that cared to notice that I was every bit as esteemed as my other teammates. During every drill, every scrimmage, on every hit, clothesline tackle, and every pass breakup, my expectations of myself had increased. No longer was I playing with that chip weighing me down. I was as carefree as my days on that thin strip of grass in front of Chollas Elementary. That meant no-holds-barred.

15 | Tokyo or Bust

The Coca-Cola Classic was an NCAA college football game played using regular-season scheduled games played in Tokyo, Japan. The series was sponsored by the popular soft drink and played from 1986 to 1993. Because the game was merely a relocation of a regular-season game, it was not considered a traditional, post-season bowl game. Bowl game or not, as a senior, I wasn't trying to miss out on the experience. A few weeks before my team's scheduled departure for Japan, I found myself on the consequence end of a poor decision.

It was a chess game of sorts. I made the first move. My professor granted me a one-day extension to turn in an assignment that accounted for half of my final grade. I had until 5:00 p.m. to turn in that paper and was in no academic position to blow it off. By 2:30 p.m., the time that I would normally head to the stadium for practice, the paper wasn't finished. I had a choice to make: keep plugging away at the term paper and miss practice or turn it in as is. I chose to skip practice and to slide my paper under the professor's door before the building closed, just minutes before 5:30 p.m. The problem was that I didn't call to tell the coaching staff what was going on. I suppose that I could have come up with some story. In hindsight, that's exactly what I should have done, but I didn't go through the trouble. I was a student-athlete facing a deadline. Any coach would understand the gravity of that situation, or so I reasoned. It was one of those times where I thought it was better to beg for forgiveness than to ask for permission.

The next day, I explained my dilemma and my choice to an unsympathetic head coach. Coach Snyder told me that I was setting a bad example for my younger teammates. Then he hit me with a bombshell.

"I'm going to have you sit out for this week's game," he said.

What! Sitting out meant missing the Big Game against Stanford. My face showed my shock. There was no hiding it. I was stunned, but I couldn't say a word. In my opinion, the punishment did not fit the crime. The Big Game decided football bragging rights between Cal and Stanford. A win could almost salvage a losing season. A decisive play could turn an unknown player into a legend. The Big Game was that important.

Because I was a captain, the coach expected me to lead by example.

"You won't play against Stanford, but you need to be there on the sidelines supporting your teammates. You do that, and we'll see about Japan," Coach Snyder said.

It was my move, and I needed to make one that would put me in a winning position. So I pretended to understand and didn't argue. Hey, I made my bed, and I had to lie in it. Swallowing a bottle of cod liver oil couldn't have been worse. The Stanford game was two days later. The Coca-Cola Classic in Tokyo was the following week. At that time, I had never traveled overseas. Whatever I had to do to make that trip, even it if meant straightening up and flying right, I was prepared to do.

That Saturday, I rode the bus to Palo Alto with my other teammates, those that didn't make the traveling squad. I felt like a chump. There I was, a senior and captain no less, rolling to the game on the bus with redshirt freshman and sophomores. I may as well have ridden the bus with the student body. During the ride, player after player asked me why I wasn't suiting up. "I'm sitting this one out," was all I could muster. Nobody knew the real reason, except the coaches and me.

There were nearly seventy-five thousand fans filling Stanford

Stadium that day. And there I was, sitting on the sidelines wearing street clothes and my letterman jacket. The most I could do was wish my teammates luck and pace the sidelines. I pumped up the crowd and slapped my teammates on their backsides during the entire game. I was visibly supportive. I went above and beyond the call of duty, posturing to impress the coaches that I was a model teammate. I endured the sights and sounds of the game—the roar of the crowd, the plays on the field—in the best way I could. In the end, my cheerleading didn't make a bit of a difference on that warm November afternoon. Cal was pounded 31–7. My playing wouldn't have made a bit of a difference, but I sure would have felt better to have been in the game fighting the good fight with my teammates.

During the bus back to Berkeley, I stewed in my prison of silence. Sitting alongside my teammates in my street clothes made my temporary demotion feel even worse. I rested my forehead against the cold, tinted glass window. Eyes glazed over, I tried to zone out the noisy chatter. It was a painful ending to a painful day. I only hoped I had done enough cheerleading to allow me to travel to Tokyo.

ON BOARD

The chartered plane stopped in Seattle en route to Tokyo to pick up our opponents, the Washington State Cougars. My team sat in the back half of the plane, and the Cougars settled into the front of the cabin. Both teams' cheerleaders were on board as well. After buckling up, I rested my head back into the luxury seat and breathed a sigh of relief because I made the trip. It wasn't my first plane ride, but at age twenty-one, it was my most memorable to date. I walked onto the chartered plane with fifty-nine of my teammates. Settling into the oversized caramel-colored leather seats, I noticed the gold-plated label on the armrest. It was the name of a Seattle Seahawks player. We were actually on the plane used by an NFL team. *This is too cool!*

The long ride was pin-drop quiet. Every player wore his best game face. We were all doing the tough, macho thing. But given the location and the expense, I guess it was necessary.

When we arrived in Tokyo, we toured a shrine and other historic attractions. Other days were spent watching game film in the hotel and practicing at the Yokohama Stadium. In the evenings, when we were given a couple hours of free time to do sightseeing and hang out, we went wild, stomping through the city like giants in the land of small people. If I felt tall at five ten, many of my teammates must have felt like Gulliver in Lilliput. The phone booths, ceilings, tubs, even the Coke cans seemed miniature.

The night before our battle, both teams enjoyed a feast. The spread of food and Coca-Cola products seemed to go for miles. I must have downed four or five little cans of Coke. To top off the night, the Miami Dolphin cheerleaders performed during the banquet dinner. I was in hog heaven. Despite the feast and fun, our clowning was confined to our section of the banquet hall. We nodded politely to the players from Washington State and prepared for the battle ahead.

The following morning was game day. November 28, 1987, I was mentally and physically ready to play. I had performed pregame drills with my teammates to cheers from Japanese fans excited to see American football up close. Whenever I leaped to catch a ball, the crowd erupted. I was pumped for battle. Ultimately, those warm-up drills would be the only opportunity I'd have to break a sweat. Coach sat me out the entire game. Apparently, I was still in the doghouse.

When the contest ended, we posted the only tie in the history of the Classic. The final score was 17–17. All was good. There was no beef to be had with the players from Washington State. That night, we all went out and partied together. It was our last night in Tokyo, and we were determined to make the most of it. More than one hundred players strong, we were American giants that took over downtown Tokyo. We hopped from club to club. We drank, danced, and carried on like we had little to no home training. Occasionally, we would run into the coaches, out enjoying the town. We'd avoid them, or they'd avoid us. But for the most part, we were off enjoying our free hall pass.

My night heated up when a teammate and I met two females at a jazz club. My friend hooked up with a sister from the States who made her living singing Anita Baker standards. Her best friend, my date, was a pretty Japanese native and spoke no English. But that fact didn't much matter. Back at their apartment, I discovered that some personal interactions are universal and require few words. We hung out way past our midnight curfew. We couldn't have cared less. It was the last game of the season. And for me, it was my last time in a football uniform.

STALEMATE

Just weeks before the Tokyo trip, a defensive coach barked out words during a goal-line stand during practice.

"C'mon, son! Push yourself! You're a senior. You don't have much longer to play this game. And I guarantee you're gonna miss it when it's over," Coach Marinelli yelled.

The coach was right. His prophetic words would grow in value with each passing year and haunt my dreams. I continue to relive highlights and missed opportunities from my playing days at Cal. I miss staring into the determined eyes of teammates during huddles, breaking up passes, and tackling players in games against UCLA or USC alongside future pro-bowl linebackers Ken Harvey and Hardy Nickerson. I also reflect fondly on the taste of the large, red, crisp apple handed to me by Washington Huskies cheerleaders as we ran off of the practice field on the Friday before the game.

Sometimes I relive the limousine bus ride through bright red and orange leaves scattered on roads in Knoxville on a beautiful autumn day, heading to play the Volunteers of Tennessee, and the police escort from the Claremont Hotel to Memorial Stadium for home games. And yes, even now I can hear the shouting of coaches and the blowing of whistles during practice in my dreams, or Lynn Swann holding the microphone for ABC Sports while pregame coverage of our contest against UCLA played at the historic Rose Bowl in Pasadena.

There are countless snippets of practice and game experiences that are cataloged in my subconscious. Time and again, these past experiences are awakened when I recognize a former coach on the NFL sidelines, like Ollie Wilson with San Diego, Ron Marinelli with

Dallas, or on television, like Steve Mariucci, an analyst with the NFL network. Those memories visit me when I least expect them, even today, nearly thirty years later. No matter what the trigger, inevitably I find myself dreaming of moments during my improbable four-year athletic, educational, and spiritual journey of a lifetime as a player on the Cal football team. Regardless of what others may believe, by the only measure that matters—mine—it was indeed the big time.

Despite being dissed by the coaching staff, the whole experience was worth the price of admission. Fortunately, I had learned how to play the politics well enough to make the trip abroad to Tokyo. Coach made an example of me, I guess, and I earned an A-minus on my term paper. By my estimation, the chess match was a stalemate.

My first trip abroad proved to be more than a chess game. It marked a quiet ending to a football career unheralded by external accounts. But for me, the experience was priceless and in many ways prepared me to be a player in another field.

My first-grade school picture, 1971. That year I was suspended and carried home for kicking my teacher.

A rough looking gang of friends at Meade Elementary School in San Diego. That's me on far right. I was about 6 years old.

My official modeling agency headshot that got me booked for
three national commercials, all while I was 12 years old.

My 11th-grade varsity football photo, Crawford High School, 1981.

Wrestling team captain and CIF champion as
a senior, Crawford High School, 1982.

Running the 110 high hurdles as a senior in a dual
meet against our rival Hoover High School.

Looking fresh after taking off my graduation garb following the
commencement ceremony at Golden Hall, downtown San Diego, June 1983.

Doing my best mean mug for my senior Cal Football photo in 1987.

Tipping my sunglasses (top, right) for the chill photo shoot of the
Cal Football defensive backs. California Memorial Stadium, 1987.

After a scrimmage during Cal Football summer training camp in Santa
Rosa, CA. Pictured with the late Rey Nicholas (left) and Dexter Jones (right).

Me next to future four-time NFL Pro Bowl linebacker
Ken Harvey (third from left) during a punt return. Cal vs.
Pacific at California Memorial Stadium, September 1987.

Me (second from left) and Cal Football teammates arriving
at the airport in Tokyo, Japan to play Washington State
in the Coca Cola Bowl. I almost missed the trip.

Here I am examining a woman while on a health mission in Mutare, Zimbabwe in 1991. I was a second-year medical student at the time.

At the Charles R. Drew medical school graduation ceremony with my siblings: LaSalle, Jaeneen, and Marvin, June 1994.

One of the proudest days of my life: graduating medical school. I'm standing with my mentor, then President of Charles R. Drew University, Dr. Reed V. Tuckson.

Celebrating my accomplishments with my mom and
secret weapon, during the Drew medical school banquet
where I gave the keynote speech that evening.

The founding members of the New York Hospital Internal
Medicine residency program's Minority Housestaff Committee
at historic Sylvia's Soul food restaurant in Harlem, NY, 1994.
Pictured (left side): me, Shelia, Raymond, and Carla.

MHC founding members. Pictured (from center to right):
Henri, Sandra, Michelle, guest, Joe, guest, and Cynthia.

I'm finally a senior resident in the New York Hospital's internal medicine program. I was still required to wear a short white coat.

Dr. Bob Fullilove has been my mentor since my early days at UC Berkeley. Here we are the American Public Health Association's annual meeting in 1999.

With my daughters (Lalah, Baele, and Maysa) at Stabroek
market in Georgetown, Guyana, soon after arriving
to start my two-year diplomatic post in 2007.

With then President of Guyana Bharrat Jagdeo (center) and former
US Ambassador to Guyana John Jones (right) at a 2008 reception to
thank members of the US military for their humanitarian assistance.

While heading the CDC office in Guyana, I cared for patients during a weekly medical clinic. Here I am at Georgetown Public Hospital with members of the surgical team in 2009.

Me delivering the "State of the Association" address at the National Association of County & City Health Officials' Annual Meeting, 2015.

PART 4
WHITE-COAT MIND-SET

16 | Eye on the Prize

Several of my teammates, some about as talented as me, went through the paces for NFL scouts. They sprinted and jumped, shuffled and lifted weights with high hopes of being invited to the NFL Combine, a place where top college players showcase their speed, strength, and football instincts through numerous drills. I watched from the bleachers at Memorial Stadium as three- and four-year starters tried to make their childhood dreams a reality. My dream was not to play in the NFL. My dream, however, was perhaps equally as ambitious and a long shot. But it was a dream that I felt I had a chance of achieving. My dream was to become a player in the field of medicine.

Students every year enter colleges and universities around the world carrying the hopes and dreams of their families along with them. They decide, sometimes naïvely, that they are destined to become something important. Parents fuel their children's ambitions. Of course, they want to tell their adult friends that their son or daughter is studying to become a doctor, an engineer, or something else that sounds impressive. Students simply fall in line and try to give their folks what they want. No one enters college with the goal of simply finishing.

For me, there was no such pressure. Since my parents hadn't graduated college by the time I entered, as a family we were just happy to be there. But I was never one for squandering opportunities. As my time as a student-athlete waned, I had to firm up my plan to become a doctor by taking the steps to make that happen. Choosing so-called premed courses was the easy part. Surviving them was another challenge altogether. Chemistry, physics, calculus, and other subjects did not interest me. I much preferred philosophy, art, and human anatomy, courses that sparked my creativity. But I had no choice. Like every other undergrad hoping to get into medical school, I had to jump through the hoops required by the American Association of Medical Colleges.

Like many incoming premed students, I thought, *Who wants to take all of those difficult useless courses?* As it turned out, I did, but only because they were a means to an end. So I fit in the four semesters of chemistry, the two semesters of physics, the two semesters of calculus, and other odds and ends to prepare. I later learned that the profession of medicine has made itself an exclusive membership club over time. To keep the numbers entering the profession small, a series of hurdles that dissuaded the weak of heart from trying to enter the profession was created. There was no other reason to require incoming students to take coursework they'd never use.

Surviving those types of courses at Berkeley was an obvious challenge for me, but surviving the doubts of others was equally taxing. Everywhere I went, I ran into fellow students who wanted to know my major and what my plans were after graduation. When I told skeptics that I planned to attend medical school, they immediately questioned me.

"What kind of grades did you get in your sciences?" people would ask.

When I told them the truth about my Cs and Bs, most people twisted their faces and mumbled, "Well, good luck." Reading between the lines was simple enough. What they meant by that was "Yeah, good luck with that."

Most of my self-appointed critics believed, as my misguidance counselor had believed, that I had no shot. Conventional wisdom dictated that my grades were too low. The majority of students with my grades would have abandoned the prospects of going to medical school or at the very least kept their plans to themselves. It wasn't as though I shared my plans with beaming confidence. It was just that I stood firm in my conviction that I was capable and determined to push forward.

17 | Shifting

As my time as a student-athlete waned, it was time for me to shed that identity and adopt a white-coat mentality. That meant visualizing myself wearing a white doctor's coat. The mind-set was important, but to make the dream a reality, I had to apply and be accepted into medical school. Unfortunately, I didn't have the best academic record to put forward.

After five years at Berkeley, I had accumulated 135 credits. Some of those credits—fifteen to be exact—were essentially useless because they didn't count toward my major or graduation requirements. I did manage to take the required courses to apply for medical school, and I scraped by with a 2.7 overall GPA. That was a B-minus by Berkeley's standards. Still, it was not going to open the doors at many medical schools.

To make matters worse, I continued to encounter dream slayers outside of campus. Ironically, many of these doubters staffed health fairs and medical school recruitment events. Imagine that. It was always the same routine. The medical school recruiters would be so happy to see me at first. They'd all jump at the chance to engage a black male student interested in going to medical school. They courted me, hard. When I showed up, they shoved pamphlets and school information down my throat and gave me logo-embossed pens and stationery like they were running for Congress. Loaded up with freebies, I got everything but the bumper stickers.

When I told them I went to Berkeley, their smiles widened like the

Grinch who stole Christmas. It was a love fest. That is, right up until the minute I told them about my grades. That's when they dropped me like a bad habit. Some recruiters gave me a little on-the-spot advice. The approach varied, but the message was always the same: no medical school would take me with my grades. *Here we go again.* Each time, the pattern repeated.

Trying to maintain my sense of humor about the whole folly, I'd sometimes lie about my grades just to see how much sucking up to me they would do. Since I was not required to produce a transcript on the spot, I made my grades whatever I wanted. Sometimes I reported a 3.5 GPA, sometimes higher. The higher my GPA, the more sucking up they did. It was comical.

Fortunately, I discovered another pathway into medical school. I learned about a program for students in my predicament. It was a program designed to help prospective medical students strengthen their science grades. It was a one-year post-baccalaureate program and represented my last chance. Unfortunately, no sooner had I applied to this program at Berkeley's School of Public Health than I learned that the program was discontinued due to a lack of funding. My application was in, but I found myself in the general application pool for incoming graduate students. That's when I decided to campaign.

My campaign was a long shot, but I had nothing to lose. I put together a self-promotion packet that included letters of recommendation from mentors and a compelling statement of purpose outlining my goal to attend medical school and how a graduate degree in public health would help me ultimately become a better doctor. With that packet in hand, I made appointments with the gatekeepers at the school: the department chair and several senior professors in the program. They were hard-pressed to turn away a student seeking to learn more about the program. So I knew that they would meet with me. But rather than listen to their pitch, I used those informational sessions to promote myself. It was the classic bait and switch. By the end of the meetings, they had learned more about me and why they should accept me into their program than I had learned about the program.

My strategy worked. They accepted me into the program, somewhat. Not as a traditional entering student, but I was admitted as a probationary student for course work only. If I maintained a B average or better, I would be allowed to complete the program and earn a master's degree in public health. If I didn't, then I would be bounced out on my ear. That was the deal.

A year later, I earned an A-minus average, and I was good to go. Always the strategist, I added a few science courses during the second year of the program to improve my science GPA for my medical school application. I took biochemistry, anatomy, and a course called Histology, the study of tissues. I earned a B and two As in those courses, proving to myself, and hopefully prospective admission committees, that I could do the work. Obviously those three grades were not going to raise my science GPA much, but it demonstrated that I had a basic aptitude for science and that I could manage the curriculum when I put my mind to the task.

18 | Getting In

With a bit of academic momentum, a graduate school transcript, and a very definite upward trend in my science GPA, I felt confident enough to apply to medical schools. The question was where to apply. There were more than one hundred medical schools from which to choose. There were East Coast and Ivy Leagues, programs like those at Harvard and Cornell. Then there were the schools on the West Coast, like UC San Francisco, Stanford, and UCLA. And of course, there were schools in practically every state in between. My chances of getting in were greatest at the public schools in my home state of California. Public schools are cheaper than private schools, and preference is given to in-state residents. But it was also important to have options.

STRATEGY

The process of applying to medical schools back then entailed completing a universal application and ticking the boxes of schools that I wanted to receive my application. I ticked all the California schools besides Stanford. There was no way I'd go there even if they accepted me. Seven years of hating them as a college rival would not permit me to do that. Sounds petty, but some things are sacred. Harvard got a tick. Not because I had a snowball's chance in hell of getting in but because no wide-eyed kid hoping to become a doctor would pass up an opportunity to apply to the best, most prestigious medical school in the country. It was pure fantasy, I realized that, but I figured I'd go for it.

My other choices included schools in Illinois, Pennsylvania, New York, and Michigan. Rounding out my list were the four historically black medical schools: Howard in DC, Meharry Medical College in Nashville, Morehouse College in Atlanta, and Charles R. Drew University of Medicine and Science in Los Angeles. All totaled, I applied to twenty-eight programs. The transcript, general application, personal statement, and one check for $150 were all put into the mail. My fate was in God's hands.

When a school had an interest in me, they sent me a secondary application that was specific to their program. These usually required short essay questions to answer, a request for a photo, and an opportunity to, as they put it, "address any inconsistencies in your performance," or to "tell the committee why you would be a good addition to the entering class."

My strategy was to turn those secondary applications around as quickly as possible. I figured that the admissions window was a small one, and I didn't want my paperwork dragging in late, landing me at the bottom of the pile. I didn't have that luxury given my average grades.

The Harvard fantasy abruptly ended when they asked for some outrageous fee to be returned along with their secondary application. It was probably Harvard's way to discourage marginal students from applying. It worked on me. Cash-strapped, that was the last they heard from me.

Along with secondary applications, I began to receive rejection letters. Cornell, UCLA, Vanderbilt, University of Pennsylvania, Meharry, and Columbia University were among the first schools not interested in me. But Pennsylvania State, University of Southern California, Boston University, and others were on board. It was a process of attrition and elimination. For every closed door, there was a glimmer of hope for the schools that had not yet rejected me. As I charted every correspondence, I watched my odds shrink week after week.

After completing and returning all of the secondary applications, I waited to see if I would be invited out for an interview. That was the third cut and, without question, the most important cut. Making it to the interviews meant that I was a legitimate contender and one step closer to my dream.

As the weeks went by, I continued to perform well in graduate school but with a steady eye toward my ultimate dream—and my mailbox. Every day I would check the mail, hold my breath, and update my tracking sheet. Some schools rejected me straight away, other schools after receiving my responses to their secondary application. But slowly the invitations for interviews began to come in one by one. Then the most remarkable thing happened. On January 19, 1990, I was admitted into medical school without an interview. The University of Illinois, College of Medicine, admitted students based solely on their secondary applications. And with that acceptance, I could breathe a sigh of relief and rest assured that my dream of becoming a medical doctor would come true.

In that instant, my outlook on my future changed. So did my strategy. For the first time during the entire application process, I was in the position to be selective. The shotgun approach had hit a target. No longer would I have to arrange to travel all over the place, at my expense, to sell myself. I found myself doing something that I never thought I'd do. I began to withdraw my application from programs, narrowing my scope in search of the place that would embrace my mission and me.

POKER FACE

Every aspect of getting into medical school required strategy. The interview was no different. If a school invited me out, in my mind that meant that I looked good enough on paper to get in and do the work. The biggest obstacle was explaining away the hiccups in my grades. Even if they didn't ask, I had to go there. It was the elephant in the room. To persuade them that I would be a welcomed addition to their entering class, I had to defend without being defensive. I had to assert without being too aggressive. Life taught me that an aggressive black man was often equated as a militant. I had to project confidence without appearing cocky. It was quite a dance.

Rehearsing helped. I practiced out loud my responses to what I knew would be obvious questions. As my interviews progressed, I developed the ability to think on my feet. Whether I sat in front of a stiff individual or a smiling panel, I learned to read my audience. During the first ten minutes, I could tell if they were buying, selling, or window-shopping. Most interviewers were not very good at hiding their impressions of me. Small facial expressions and body language provided clues. The complete nonbelievers shut down almost immediately. My fans, on the other hand, were eating out of the palm of my hand in no time. They began selling the school to me, rather than the reverse.

"I think that you would be happy here," they'd say. "We have excellent student support services here," they'd continue to sell.

The wheels in their head began tumbling, thinking to themselves that they were about to snag me. I wasn't the strongest applicant, but then again a B-minus average from UC Berkeley was nothing to sneeze at, especially for midrange programs wanting to boost their numbers of minority students. Having earned both my bachelor's and master's degrees from Cal, I was a relatively rare commodity. The more I interviewed, the more this became apparent to me.

With a solid offer in hand, I received invitations for a personal interview at thirteen schools across the county, from California to Massachusetts. I couldn't afford to crisscross the county to make them all. So I chose strategically to travel to six schools: three in my home state of California, one in DC, and two in Pennsylvania.

In Pennsylvania, I interviewed at Hahnemann and the Medical College of Pennsylvania. In DC, I interviewed at Howard University. And I visited the University of Southern California, UC Davis, and a joint medical education program called Charles Drew-UCLA in Los Angeles. Despite being rejected from UCLA School of Medicine, the Drew-UCLA program was still very much interested. I ranked it among my top choices.

RACE MATTERS

During my interviews, I began to notice something else oddly gratifying. It was about my hair at the time. I wore my hair in an Afrocentric style resembling kinky coils. I had done so for years, so I didn't think too much of it. It was not uncommon for my interviewer to do a double take or stare at my mane when they thought I wouldn't notice. Strangely, it seemed, my locks acted as a kind of filter. It was as if my physical appearance said what I could not: I am fully committed to maintaining a strong self-image throughout the process of learning how to become a doctor. As a black man emerging, I was not trying to remake myself. I had no desire to pass for a white person in black skin simply because I was entering one of the most respected professions. The fact that my agenda was so transparent seemed to put admissions gatekeepers on notice.

During my interview at the College of Pennsylvania in Philadelphia, I learned that the medical school was forced to build a dormitory for their black and brown students. Their newly hired minority recruiter, an African American brother, divulged that to me. He told me that many residents in the surrounding neighborhoods were reluctant to rent rooms to minority students. That caused me to be perplexed. *This can't be right. This is 1990, not 1960.* However, my personal experience with a local family made the truth more real to me. The family received payment from the medical college to temporarily house out-of-town students who came to interview. Because of my interview schedule, I stayed with them for two nights. The hospitality of my host was most unsettling, although I discovered the subtlety quite by accident. On the second morning, as I sat bent over my steaming bowl of oatmeal for the second day in a row, the couple's son ran downstairs.

"What? No blueberry muffins or eggs? Where's the big breakfast?" he asked, disappointed.

Having a guest in the house, I supposed he looked forward to a hearty breakfast on the days that medical recruits stayed in his home, especially given the fact that the medical school paid them. Instead, his mother, my ungracious host, blushing with silent embarrassment, served up mush two days in a row. Ironically, weeks later I was accepted into that school. Needless to say, I did not accept. The program did not pass my litmus test, and my host family did little to help.

My interview at Southern Cal took on a different but no less disturbing tone. There, I interviewed with an older white gentleman who proceeded to lecture me about the ills of affirmative action. It was as if I was a captive audience, and he wanted to vent all of his personal opinions about why race shouldn't matter. Minority students, he reasoned, should be held to the same high standards as every other student. If they didn't make the grade, he argued, then so be it. They didn't earn the right to be admitted. If the entering class was all white, it simply reflected the lack of qualified minority applicants and was no fault of the university, he reasoned.

"Let the chips fall where they may," he said.

Then why am I here? I thought. *The invitation that I received in the mail from your institution stated that I was a highly qualified candidate. Did I just spend good money to fly out here to hear this?* It seemed to me like nothing more than intellectualized racism.

My chips must have fallen right because I received notice a month later that I was selected for their wait-list. Nonetheless, the prospect of spending thirty thousand dollars a semester to be educated in that elitist incubator was not appealing. I was looking for a medical school that would embrace my sense of mission and identity—and one that didn't have to go out of its way to accommodate or tolerate black and brown students.

My interviews with the selection committees at Howard and Drew were very different from those at majority white institutions. Howard is located in the heart of the nation's capital. Known in many circles as the mecca of black urban life, Washington, DC, had much to offer. Drew University is located in South Central Los Angeles. Both institutions were surrounded by urban communities with much greater social needs and less healthy people, much like G Street and the surrounding communities where I grew up.

The faculty at both programs looked like me. Instead of working under professors and instructors that may have secretly despised my being at their prestigious place of higher learning, I could be nurtured under the committed tutelage of long-term faculty, purpose-driven with a focus on turning out doctors most likely to serve the neediest communities across the country. More importantly, I saw my reflection in the eyes of faculty that embraced all of me.

During my interviews at these historically black medical schools, I sat across from pioneers in the practice of urban medicine. They asked me questions about my grades just as the other institutions had, but they asked other questions too. They wanted to know what difference I hoped to make in the world as a physician. Sure, medicine was a good way to make a living, but these programs gave me the sense that it could be more than that. Their questions about making a contribution to underserved communities gave me a sense that beyond a job, a physician could be a kind of missionary. Most significantly, though, these places, and Charles R. Drew University in particular, convinced me that I could personally make a difference.

During the spring of 1990, I was accepted into an additional four medical schools. With a half a dozen acceptances and a handful of schools wait-listing me, I chose to attend Drew University. I moved to Los Angeles and never looked back. One in a class of twenty-four students selected from nearly thirteen hundred applicants, I knew that I had found the place I was destined to be.

19 | Mountains

The room was cold and sterile. Bright fluorescent bulbs hung just below the ceiling tiles and lit up the entire room. The place smelled like a mixture of formaldehyde and cleaning products. I stood with more than a hundred anxious first-year medical students in the center of the room, awaiting instructions. It was the most anticipated class for first-year medical students: gross anatomy. High-post tables with tin domes covering lifeless cadavers were placed at twenty-five stations around the room. All of the students, including me, were on pins and needles to uncover the bodies. *What would my body look like?*

CALLED OUT

There was a buzz in the room that we would be grouped four or five persons to a body. It was not the same as having my body to cut on, I thought, but if my group was made up of people I liked, it could be just as exciting. Gradually, I squirmed my way to the front of the semicircle surrounding the anatomy professor to hear his directions. No sooner had I done that than a well-built, tall black man wearing a white lab coat entered the room. My interest was piqued as he was introduced.

"Class, I'd like to introduce Doctor Jackson. He runs our pathology laboratory and will be a great resource to you," the professor announced.

Then he invited Dr. Jackson to address the class. With his deep, booming voice, he introduced himself and began sharing some fun facts about his job and the lab. Apparently, he directed the lab that prepared many of the specimens that we would see throughout the semester. He seemed smart and charming. It looked to me like I might have found a new mentor.

"What's your name, son?" he asked, pointing right at me.

"LaMar," I said, beaming ear to ear because in a room full of chuckling students, he had singled me out.

"What kind of hairstyle is that?" he said, referring to my twists.

He caught me completely off guard. "It's my kind of style," I replied. I wondered why he was coming for me.

"And look how you're dressed, son. You don't even look like a medical student," he continued his critique of me.

"Well, I am a medical student," I replied defiantly. *What's his problem?* Embarrassed, I grew angrier by the second.

His unprovoked attack was followed by a moment of awkward silence by the entire class. It was almost as if collectively we were holding our breath, waiting for the other shoe to drop. As if he would tell us that he was just joking, and we'd all have a good laugh at my expense. But that moment never came. Instead, the class was dispersed and told to grab a station.

No one in my group questioned me about the inquisition, but silently I burned inside. *How dare he call me out like that?* I repeatedly said in my head. *What's that guy's problem?* I was determined to confront him immediately after class. But my anger consumed me so much that I couldn't even concentrate on my cadaver or the lesson at hand. I couldn't take it. It was my turn to be brave like my sister, Jaeneen, and confront the Goliath.

"Excuse me, guys. I'll be right back," I told my group.

I spotted Dr. Jackson in the corner of the room talking with our professor and decided to make a beeline to him.

"Excuse me, Doctor Jackson," I interrupted.

"Yes. Can I help you?" he replied nonchalantly, as if he hadn't clowned me in front of the entire class minutes earlier.

"Can I talk to you for a minute?" I asked.

He agreed, and I walked him outside the classroom and into the hallway. I wasted no time giving him a piece of my mind.

"I want you to know that I don't appreciate you trying to embarrass me in front of my classmates. I have every right to be here, just like these white students. I earned my bachelor's and master's at UC Berkeley and worked hard to get where I am. And by the way, if I choose to wear my hair this way, I can. Because it's not about what's on my head. It's about what's *in* my head, between my ears," I told him boldly.

He stood silent and seemed surprised at my reaction.

I continued, "I am a medical student second. But I'm a man first. And you need to treat me like a man. I'm not going to let you or anyone else disrespect me. If you want respect, you have to give respect. And what you did in there to me was disrespectful."

My words must have struck a chord because Dr. Jackson immediately apologized. He explained that he didn't intend to belittle me but that he thought it would be more appropriate to wear a shirt with a collar. He was squirming for sure. He even invited me to work in his lab when I had some spare time. I thanked him, but quietly I had no intention of working with him. That bridge was burnt before it was even built. Besides, there were two things that I had little of: one was spare time; the other was patience for what seemed to be an arrogant Uncle Tom faculty member that tried to invalidate my purpose.

SURVIVAL TACTICS

In addition to gross anatomy, there were other time-demanding subjects. The books that I had to buy were all four inches thick. Like most competitive programs, students projected confidence even during the times when they were completely overwhelmed. There were a select few students that figured out how to study in groups and push through the material relatively unscathed. We called them gunners. They sat at the front of the lecture hall, shooting up their hand to answer every question, irritating the hell out of the rest of us. They walked around with an air of superiority like their cadaver didn't stink. But from what I could tell, the majority of us mere mortal medical students were buried under mountains of things, like volumes of textbooks, lab manuals, lecture notes, and the box of skeleton bones on loan from the anatomy lab. On top of that, it was important to try to squeak out a social life. Striking the proper balance wasn't always easy.

Finding a study partner or kindred spirit made things much more bearable. I eventually bonded with a brother from Oakland, California, named Ernie. Oak-town Ernie, as I came to call him, was secure in himself, down to earth, open to friendship, and hilarious. Everyone liked Ernie, and many of us came to rely on the clever mnemonics that he invented for remembering scientific facts. He was brilliant when it came to stuff like that. Most of the minority students in the first-year class at UCLA were in the twenty-four-member Drew-UCLA program—most but not all. There were five African American brothers, including me, out of the entire 150-member class at UCLA. Three of us were in the Drew program. Ernie was not. It didn't matter. What was important for me was to have at least someone I could relate to when confronted with so much stuff to learn. Ernie and I didn't do too much direct studying together, but we provided mutual moral support in a way that was real and noncompetitive.

Stressing about grades was necessary because a C-grade wasn't considered acceptable. Students were permitted to earn one, maybe two Cs, but an overall C-average usually resulted in a student having to repeat the semester.

I didn't worry much about not passing. During the early part of the semester, I was enjoying the Southern California sun and the beautiful Westwood community, riding around in my drop-top convertible VW Cabriolet. My confidence was bolstered by the fact that I had a graduate degree, academic momentum, and I had taken histology, a first-year medical school course, the year before at Berkeley and had earned an A-minus grade. That fact allowed me to be one of a handful of tutors for that course. It also essentially guaranteed me an A.

Similar to my undergraduate days, I tended to study solo. Every now and again, I would borrow notes from one of my classmates, but most often I was tucked away in the stacks at the UCLA medical library all alone, burning the midnight oil as time drew closer to exams. Help came in the form of student-run reviews before exams and the bathroom stalls during the exams. Some students would take advantage of their bathroom break during exams. They would disappear into the stalls for about ten minutes where they could review their crib notes hidden in the paper dispenser or toilet cover dispenser. Obviously, with time ticking, and with only one trip allowed, it required a fast review. But for some students, every point counted, and every little bit helped.

When the first semester came to an end, I boasted a solid academic record. Not stellar but solid. That was reassuring for me because, in addition to studying, I was voted class president for the first-year Drew-UCLA program. Even though Drew students were integrated into the larger UCLA medical program, we still did a few things separate and apart. For example, once a month Dr. Singleton, the assistant dean for student affairs at Drew, held a meeting for us on the UCLA campus in Westwood. We had our own class officers, newsletter, and student meetings. Other than that, for the first two years, students in the Drew program were indistinguishable from other UCLA medical students.

Black, proud, and on a mission, I always felt special to be a member of the Drew class, even if some of my Drew classmates tried to distance themselves from the perceived stigma associated with a program focused on the medical needs of the underserved. Personally, I couldn't wait for year three when I'd start my rotations at the Los Angeles County-Martin Luther King Jr. Hospital located in the heart of Watts. By design, Drew students practiced clinical medicine in the hood rather than the UCLA-affiliated hospitals in the more affluent areas in Los Angeles.

ON THE BUBBLE

Being promoted from one year to the next proved to be more than just a notion. Even with Ernie as a homeboy, Kevin, a second-year student assigned to me as a mentor, solitary study, and the occasional notes from a few classmates like Tonya and Suzanne, I still fell woefully short. It eventually caught up with me.

"What do you mean?" I asked in desperation.

"I mean it doesn't look like the promotion committee is going to move you on. You failed both neurology and biochemistry. They are going to recommend that you repeat," Dr. Singleton said with a disappointed tone.

Dr. Singleton was not the kind to mince words, so I knew the situation was serious.

"Can't I take make-up exams or something?" I asked in a panic. "There must be something I can do." I held my breath.

"Well, you can always plead your case to the promotions committee. They may allow you to retake the final exams, but I can't make you any promises," she replied.

"Yes. I want to plead my case. But wait. What about my research fellowship that starts in a few weeks? I won't be here," I said.

Dr. Singleton paused for a moment and then said, "You go on to Atlanta. Write a statement. I'll have it read on your behalf. That's the best we can do."

I jumped right on it and pounded out the most compelling statement of explanation that I could. My letter to the promotions committee was so compelling that they accepted my proposal. They allowed me to take make-up exams in both subjects, but I had to pass them with an A-grade. If I did that, I would be allowed to continue with my class as a second-year medical student. If not, then I would be required to repeat my first year. They also stipulated that there would be an oral exam for neurology as well as the written test.

It was no simple feat. To complete a ten-week infectious diseases summer fellowship at the Centers for Disease Control and Prevention in Atlanta, Georgia, in eight weeks took my best efforts. My days were spent under the laboratory hood performing the delicate work of cellular immunology, trying to advance the understanding of how HIV, the virus that causes AIDS, attaches to healthy cells before entering and destroying them. The work was stimulating, important, and held the promise for vaccine development. My nights, on the other hand, were dedicated to studying. For about three hours every night, I pushed through the tiresome task of relearning biochemistry and neurology, two subjects unrelated to my research for the summer but crucial for my promotion in medical school. Eight weeks was all I had to prepare for my exams, complete my research, and give a presentation to the entire CDC fellowship class and their supervisors.

With my back against the wall, I tried to be as organized as possible. And with each passing week, as I plowed through chapter after chapter, my stack of index cards grew. *I can do this. I've got to do this. No way will I be left behind. I'd lose an entire year.*

The fear of failure was all the motivation I needed to keep pushing. Thinking about my classmates moving on to their second year and me running into them in the hallways as a repeating first-year student made me sick to my stomach. I channeled that sick feeling into study techniques to help me master the material. I drew diagrams, wrote detailed outlines, and reviewed my growing stack of note cards twice a day. It was hard to know when enough studying was enough. It was not until I faced my two neurology professors for my oral exam that I had my first inclination.

"Can you describe what we would expect to see on an EEG of a person with a seizure?" one professor asked.

Immediately I recognized that he was referring to the electroencephalogram tracing of someone with epilepsy. That picture was etched into my brain because I had drawn it so many times over the summer.

"Well, the classic tracing is a spike-and-wave pattern. It's seen most commonly in absence epilepsy or petit mal seizure. Would you like me to draw it?" I said without hesitation.

The look on his face told the story. He was more than impressed; he was surprised. He nodded to the other professor before responding.

"You're exactly right. I don't think we've had any student answer that question correctly. No, no, you don't need to draw it," he said.

That's when I knew that my summer preparation was enough. It took another day for the scores on my written tests to be tallied, but I already knew that I had made the grades I needed to continue as a second-year student. Two of my classmates weren't as lucky. They were forced to repeat the first year.

When I entered medical school for my second year, I felt golden. Starting year two for most returning students was routine business following the summer break. But for me, having survived the scare of being held back, I had a greater appreciation for my position as a second-year medical student. Being promoted from one year to the next was not a foregone conclusion, not anymore. I learned that the hard way. As a result, I took care to mind my studies and make the grades needed to progress.

20 | King Me

"Wake up! Wake up!" I shouted at the top of my lungs.

It was just like that scene in Spike Lee's movie *School Daze*. And I felt like the character Dap, frustrated and angry. Los Angeles was burning up, and so was I. It was April 1992, and I was a medical student in the spring semester of my second year. It was the day after the Rodney King verdict, and the city riots were swelling to peak intensity. Students on the UCLA campus held a rally to express their concerns. The looting and burning hadn't spread to Westwood, but every student, like every American, I would imagine, was affected. There was a palpable tension that engulfed the city like a dark cloud. When I reached for the megaphone in front of several thousand students, I had no idea what I would say. I just knew that I had to raise my voice and say something. What came out of my mouth next, I could not have predicted.

"Wake up!" I repeated that statement at the top of my lungs about five times and then paused long enough to catch my breath and witness the drama of the silenced crowd. Then I spoke my truth by recounting the story that had taken place a week earlier.

A friend and I had arranged to meet somewhere in Orange County. He drove south from Los Angeles, and I drove north from San Diego. It was a quick meeting that took place just off the freeway exit for me to grab my wallet that I had dropped in his car by mistake. Neither of us wanted to drive the entire 130 miles, so we agreed to meet somewhere in the middle. While legally parked on the side of the road near a gas station, I grabbed my wallet, and then we began to reminisce about our fun-filled weekend in San Diego. The weekend was part of what had become a yearly pilgrimage for the Pros and Coaches Anti-drug Campaign, a scholarship and youth program created by our mutual friend and my high school buddy, Rudy. For ten years, we handed out scholarships, met with inner-city youth, renewed friendships with other folks and guest speakers that traveled out for the event, and partied.

Chucky and I couldn't have been chatting for more than ten minutes when it happened. Bright blue flashing lights appeared out of nowhere. Within thirty seconds, we were surrounded by five police cars. Alarmed, I wondered what law we had broken. *Is this a case of mistaken identity?*

Several cops sprung out of their cars, some with their hands on their holsters, and approached us.

"I need you to put your hands on the trunk of the car. Now!" a cop shouted.

As I sat in the back of the car, I began to assess the situation, trying to view things through the eyes of police officers from an affluent, mostly white, conservative place like Orange County. Then it dawned on me what our crime was: DWB, driving while black. Chucky and I were handcuffed and put in separate police cruisers. *This is racial profiling. No doubt about it.*

Someone, probably some do-gooders at the nearby gas station, had reported us. Two young black men, with nice cars, standing on the side of the road, talking, had to be up to no good. It was probably reported as a drug deal in progress. My hunch was confirmed when I saw the police and the drug-sniffing dogs search my parents' black 740 Volvo Turbo and Chucky's white Mercedes Benz, 500 series.

"Whose car is this?" the officer leaned into the police car to ask me.

"It's my parents'," I said.

He then showed me a Ziploc bag filled with white capsules.

"And what's in here?" he pressed, as if he had busted me.

I replied promptly, "I don't know, probably my parents' garlic pills."

My parents were vegetarians and took herbal supplements all the time, so I was certain about my answer.

As I sat with my arms pinned behind my back, I wondered about my fate. I looked over at Chucky locked down in another car, and I knew he must have been thinking the same thing. His eyes were sad, like mine. Victims, we were trapped at the unjust nexus of racial prejudice and probable cause, our freedom revoked, and powerless. And with the racially charged Rodney King trial dominating the news, the timing could not have been worse.

After being illegally detained for more than an hour, Chucky and I were released. We nodded to each other and drove our separate ways. For the entire drive back, I thought about what I had just gone through and how much worse it could have been. Stories about rogue cops shooting first and asking questions later and the growing accounts of police brutality were being reported across the country. There I was, a second-year medical student no less, with more formal education than the cops that pulled me over, and it didn't matter. It didn't matter that Chucky was a family man and longtime Los Angeles city employee. It didn't matter that neither one of us had a criminal record. We were victimized simply for being black in that space and time.

"That's not right, and I'm tired of it!" I yelled at the rally after I recounted the events of that night. "These rogue cops are getting away with murder, literally, and we're just supposed to stand by and take it," I yelled. "That's what happened to Rodney King. Only this time someone happened to be videotaping it. That's why my message today is to wake up. Wake up!"

When I handed the megaphone back to the rally organizer, the crowd went wild with cheers. My heart pounded, and my body trembled, partly because I relived my traumatic ordeal and partly because I realized that I could have been Rodney King on the side of the road, beaten within an inch of my life.

TRAFFIC STOP

Classes at UCLA were canceled on that day. The university administration gave students a day to decompress. For me, it was the first time that I had openly vented my hurt and frustration from the DWB incident. After hanging at the rally for nearly two hours, I jumped in my car and headed home. Stuck in traffic, I started to get frustrated all over again.

What's taking this guy so long to move?

I stuck my head out of my window to try to see who was in front of me driving like Miss Daisy. *It figures. An Asian driver. What a surprise,* I thought to myself. It was a racist thing to say, I know, but at that moment, everything seemed to be about race.

I began to lean on my horn. *Maybe if I honk at him long enough, he'll get moving.* But it didn't seem to help. Finally, fed up, I jumped out of my car, slammed my car door shut, and walked up to the driver's side door to protest.

"What's your problem? Why won't you move this car? Can't you see I'm trying to get somewhere?" I asked.

The small Asian man shrugged and tried to explain that the problem was the congestion in front of him. At that moment, I felt guilty—ashamed. Who was I to get out of my car and confront a stranger? That wasn't me. Never in my life had I acted so inappropriately or irresponsibly. The racial animosity ignited by the King verdict spread like a disease, and I was infected. Still, that was no excuse.

When I came to my senses and turned to go back to my car, I was confronted by another infected person. A white man jumped out of his car to confront me, presumably for holding up traffic. Only he had a tire iron in his hand. Before I could say anything, he raised the tire iron over his head and came toward me.

"Whoa, whoa!" I said, panicked as I backed up.

My words were apparently enough to snap him back to his senses because he immediately lowered his weapon and headed back to his car, mumbling profanities the entire way.

A black man, an Asian man, and a white man, normally

coexisting civilly, interacting under the black cloud of heightened racial tensions during a routine traffic jam became a combustible situation. Unfortunately, on the heels of the King verdict, these types of situations were popping up all over LA, often with more disastrous outcomes. It was the same anger that led to the attack on Reginald Denny, a white truck driver stopped at the intersection of Florence and Normandie Avenues who was dragged from his vehicle and severely beaten with a brick to his head by a mob of local black residents one day earlier. It was the kind of rage that led to widespread and unchecked looting and fires across Los Angeles, and open gun battles between armed mobs and Korean American shopkeepers trying to defend their livelihoods.

The riots, with widespread looting, assault, arson, and murder, lasted for six days, ending after soldiers from the Army National Guard along with US Marines from Camp Pendleton were called in to stop the rioting. In total, fifty-three people were killed, two thousand people were injured, and property damages, including nearly 3,800 burned buildings, topped $1 billion.

A tire iron or a brick. Being dragged out of a car at an intersection or choosing to jump out. But for the grace of God, I could have been caught up in a bad way, and being an educated black man with promise would not have made a bit of difference. Thankfully, even as the city began the process of healing and rebuilding, I was able to retreat behind the walls of the academy, but I chose to stay involved. I was one of a handful of medical students and faculty that organized the South Central Youth Congress, a day-long program dedicated to helping high school students find healthy, nonviolent ways to vent their hurt and expedite the rebuilding of their communities. My focus renewed, I channeled my energy into finishing medical school and prayed that the words of Rodney King to "all just get along" would resonate with city dwellers and students alike.

21 | Finishing

After two years on the Westwood campus, I migrated with my fellow classmates in the Drew-UCLA program to South Central Los Angeles to begin my clinical rotations. Arriving at the Martin Luther King-Charles R. Drew campus was liberating. It was what I had looked forward to since entering the program. Finally, I was at the center of the action where, even as a medical student, I felt I was desperately needed. It was time to put the book learning acquired during the first two years to the test.

Drew students were required to spend their entire third year at the King-Drew Medical Center, a five-hundred-bed teaching hospital with a very active Level 1 trauma center, located between the Compton and Watts neighborhoods. King-Drew cared for some of the sickest and poorest residents in Los Angeles County. My time was spent in the hospital learning real-life medicine during four- to eight-week intervals called rotations. It didn't take long for me to appreciate why the place had earned the nickname "Killer King." It did so partly because of the perceived poor quality that patients received at any county hospital in Los Angeles, partly because so many patients came to the place on death's door, and partly because it was located in a high crime area of the city, where gunshot wounds were commonplace. In fact, King-Drew treated so many GSWs that the US military sent their trauma surgeons there for hands-on training.

Within no time, I jumped right in as a part of the health care team. It wasn't long before I was holding retractors during open surgery or inserting large needles into the chest of trauma victims to vent the air surrounding a collapsed lung. Reading dilated pupils, drawing blood gases, and inserting central lines into the neck and groin areas of patients to administer lifesaving fluids became almost second nature for me.

Real patients were nothing like the cold, lifeless cadavers that I dissected in gross anatomy lab. These were living, sometimes dying, organisms struggling for life. They resembled people that I knew. The gurgling, sighing, whistling sounds that came out of their bodies were proof positive that even as life was ebbing away, people did all within their power to cling to what was left of it. Their stories could sometimes be read through their scars, body piercings, or tattoos. Some of the saddest stories were of innocent lives struck down in the flower of youth. Standing by as my supervising doctor told family members that their loved one couldn't be saved was heartbreaking, but I learned to express sympathy with composure.

ROTATIONS

It wasn't all death. As a third-year medical student, I made my way through each clinical rotation and experienced new worlds of science and wonder. During my four weeks on the obstetrics rotation, I pulled life from the wombs of a dozen women while spending long hours on the labor and delivery ward, constantly checking expected mothers as they ripened through the night. Sometimes I broke their water to speed things along. When the mother's cervix was fully dilated, I would wheel her into the delivery suite. Adrenaline pumping, I would slip on my gown, take my position at the foot of the bed, and guide the infant out of womb, first the head, then one shoulder at a time. It was exhausting and exhilarating.

Pediatrics was all about comforting parents. In many cases, that almost seemed more important than comforting the sick child, because short of catastrophic illness, most kids had the resiliency to bounce back from almost anything, or so it seemed to me. Whereas pediatrics tested my patience, surgery tested my stamina and focus. Holding clamps and retractors motionless for hours at a time, blood pooling in my feet and muscles nearly cramping, required discipline of a physical type. Answering questions about organ functions and identifying anatomical landmarks in an open body required mental sharpness. Enough correct answers during the course of the operation earned me the privilege of suturing the body closed. As a medical student, that was considered a big payoff.

A young, strong, able-bodied man, I never had a reason to consider the fragility of the human mind. There was no one that I knew personally who suffered from mental illness. But after sitting in on group counseling sessions and walking the psychiatry wards, that all changed. Learning about depression, bipolar disease, paranoid schizophrenia, and OCD in books was one thing. Seeing disoriented human forms walking aimlessly in circles, draped in hospital gowns, with their naked backsides out, mumbling to themselves, was something altogether different. Witnessing various states of psychological imbalance was jarring. Considering that my biggest fear, even in my darkest hour, was that I might have to repeat a year of medical school, my concerns paled in comparison to those patients struggling to make sense out of the basic affairs of daily life.

My third year was a journey of eye-opening discoveries. Every rotation taught me about clinical medicine and about myself, the world around me, and the beauty and ugliness of life. By witnessing the joy of birth, the sorrow of death, the vulnerability of the sick, the conflicted tensions between family members fighting over the medical futility of loved ones, the arrogance of medical heroics, and the serenity of a person willing to let go, I learned constantly.

The patient-doctor relationship within the hallowed halls of the hospital was like experiencing life behind the curtain backstage. Few witnessed expressions of dependence, faith, gratitude, mistrust, fear, hope, even desperation with such purity as that shown by people putting their lives into the hands of someone (or something) else. Self-reflection was a necessary part of my process, and I embraced it and prayed a whole lot.

SENIORITIS

Never let them see you sweat. That was my mantra during my fourth year of medical school. If I lacked answers to questions about the conditions of my patients and was too embarrassed to ask out loud, I quickly looked it up during a spare moment or after I left the hospital for the day. With that strategy, along with my improving performance on exams and bedside quizzes, my confidence grew. Feeling like a real doctor, I began to sail through my senior year.

It was not as if I was mastering everything, but I felt good about my progress and good about myself. My world seemed to spin so fast that I rarely stopped to take stock of my station in life. There I was, a kid from the deficit environment of G Street who somehow managed to push past the doubters and misguidance counselors to navigate the academic rigors of UC Berkeley, and who circumvented self-doubt to make it to my senior year in medical school. But even as I was becoming increasingly comfortable in my own skin, I repeatedly encountered black folks who seemed to be uncomfortable not only with their own sense of identity but with mine. This phenomenon vexed me. But I never expected what happened to me on that fateful afternoon.

In so many ways, it was a perfect day. Sunny in Los Angeles, I had the weekend off and nothing to do but personal errands. So I rode my bike to a local store to grab a few things. Standing just outside the automatic sliding doors of the market, I tilted my head back, closed my eyes softly, and finished my cold drink before mounting my bike to head back to my apartment. The sun felt good on my forehead and cheeks. With no particular place to go and no rush to be anywhere, I began to soft-pedal my way in the direction of home. Venice Avenue was always buzzing with traffic, so I didn't make much of the city bus that pulled alongside me at a stoplight. Nor did I notice the back window slide open. It was only when an outstretched arm waving out the window caught my peripheral vision. It was two young black brothers demanding my attention.

"Hey," the stranger said, looking down on me out of the window of the bus.

Of course I assumed that he was just trying to be friendly, so I responded with a nod and "What's up?"

"Your hair ain't shit," he responded.

Huh? What did I do to deserve that? Surprised, I decided to ignore them at that point. Surely, the Nubian twists in my hair were no affront to him, I thought. And then it happened. As the bus began to move, he repeated his unprovoked statement and then spit at me. Actually, he spit *on* me. It landed on my arm. I looked up, surprised and confused. The bus accelerated, and he laughed his head off, taunting me. It pissed me off.

The bus headed down Venice Avenue, picking up speed through every intersection, and I gave chase. Powered by determined legs and pure anger, I pedaled as fast as I could. I came close a few times, usually when the bus stopped at a light or bus stop, but the bus would start moving again, and I would fall behind. My resolve to get to my attacker grew stronger with every block I measured. When I got one stop ahead of the bus, I would throw down my bike, step onto the bus, bypass paying the fare, and streak right to the back of the bus and shake the stew out of that guy. Three miles down the road and a good eight blocks past Jasmine Avenue, the street I lived on, my legs gave out. Sweat dripped off my face, and I stood there panting as the bus drove away. Just as I turned to head back home in the opposite direction, my Saturday afternoon nemesis flipped me the bird out of his open window.

It was as if the universe conspired against me and my near-perfect day. For the life of me, I couldn't figure out why. Unfortunately, this troubling pattern would repeat itself throughout my schooling and professional development. That is, black folk rebelling against *my* expression of blackness. White people may have had their own problems with me, but I figured that was par for the course. Why a confident black man would stir the souls of other black folk was (and is to this day) something that I have yet to wrap my brain around. But I've never made it a point to apologize for being me. It was never an option.

STEPPING OUT

Testing my doctoring abilities beyond the South Central environment, I successfully completed elective rotations at the Harlem Hospital in New York City and the Boston City Hospital, and I did well in both. Then without so much as thinking twice, I elected to do a four-week cardiology rotation at the renowned Cedar-Sinai Medical Center located between Beverly Hills and West Hollywood. Cedars was a pioneer for heart valve transplants and invasive procedures for the heart, so it seemed like a good place to learn cardiology. It was my last official elective before cruising across the finish line. After completing that rotation, I planned to coast straight to graduation.

Going into my last rotation, I had a different mind-set for two reasons. For one, I was exhausted from all of the studying, like a bad case of senioritis. And two, match day was over. Probably one of the tensest days in the life of a medical student, match day is the day when seniors all across the country find out where they've been accepted to do their paid hospital training, called internship and residency. Students chose hospital programs, hospitals chose students, and the rank lists went into some elaborate national computer database. On match day, students received a sealed envelope with their highest-ranked match, and that's where they went. I matched with my number-one choice, the New York Hospital Cornell Medical Center. My future was set. So getting through the cardiology elective at Cedars was merely a formality.

Things were going about as well as could be expected until my supervising resident doctor heard about where I was accepted into residency.

"Wow. You got into the medicine program at Cornell?" he asked.

"Yep," I replied proudly.

"You know that's one of the best medicine programs in New York, right?" he questioned me as if I had accidently stumbled into the program. "How'd you get into that program?" he continued.

After his initial question, I assumed he was passively curious if not supportive. However, when he asked the follow-up question, I became insulted and realized that he was envious of my good fortune.

"I applied and interviewed like everyone else," I responded.

"Oh, well that's pretty impressive," he strained to recover, perhaps realizing that his jealousy was apparent.

No doubt, I thought.

From that moment on, the game had changed. My supervising resident ceased to be my teacher and instead became my harshest critic. He challenged me at every turn. It was like some sick competition ensued, and he was determined to prove that I wasn't so smart or deserving to be admitted into a premier medicine residency program, after all. Like a slave caught learning how to read, I felt as if I was being punished for simply trying to better myself.

"He really has it in for you. You should, you know, kiss up to him a little bit. Maybe then he'll get off your back," Steve, a senior classmate of mine in the UCLA program, suggested.

Not happening. If he has a problem with me, he'll just have to get over it, I told myself but didn't bother answering Steve. Instead, I rolled over in my upper bunk in the small on-call room for students and tried to get a wink of sleep before my pager sounded off again. Steve had no idea that I had survived far worse than an envious second-year resident. There was no way I was going to allow him to get under my skin. My plan was to do my work, keep my head down, and count down the days, hoping that the four-week rotation would fly by. There was nothing that he could do that would result in the New York Hospital program rescinding their offer. My place was secure. Given that reality, as far as I was concerned, my resident and Steve could both kick rocks.

It was apparent when I received my final grade at the completion of the rotation that my resident was determined to have the last word.

"D-minus? Are you kidding me? C'mon, Doctor Miller, I've never earned anything less than a B-grade on any clinical rotation. This guy tried to screw me!" I was outraged.

Dr. Ted Miller, dean of student affairs, gave me a look that confirmed my suspicion.

"It certainly looks that way. From the looks of the evaluation, he started to give you an F and then changed it to a D-minus," Dr. Miller answered, almost sympathetically. "He wrote here that you were dishonest and unreliable."

"Yeah, right. If I was so bad, why didn't he ever pull me aside and tell me? He's just going to watch me fail miserably for four weeks without any counseling, then fail me?" Staring at my resident's written evaluation, I couldn't believe my eyes.

Dr. Miller shook his head. He understood what had happened. He explained, "Okay, so the way I see it, you can do one of two things. You can appeal this grade, but it will probably be in vain. Or you can let it go and focus on graduating. Unfortunately, you will need to take another elective in the remaining two weeks to be eligible to graduate. It's unfortunate, I know, but sometimes you have to choose your battles."

In no position to fight another uphill battle, I conceded. Together, Dr. Miller and I identified another rotation for me to take to meet the graduation requirements. It was something I really had no interest in doing, but it was a means to an end. The best way to get back at that resident, I figured, was to graduate on time and head off to the best medicine program in New York. So that's what I did.

My last days at Drew University were not memorable for dodging the bullet of a failing grade from Cedars, or suffering through a two-week geriatric rotation, or giving the student speech at the senior banquet. It was most memorable for the talk with our university president, Dr. Reed V. Tuckson. He assembled all the seniors in a small conference room, about twenty of us. We were his third graduating class since taking the helm of the university, and he had a few choice words of wisdom to share.

"When you walk across that stage next week, I want you to understand that you take the dreams and hopes of your family and your community with you. You have earned the degree of doctor of medicine, something that very few can ever hope to attain. And if you take care of it, it will take care of you. No matter where you go, you will always be able to earn a living and put food on your table because the world will always need doctors. Never forget what you learned here and always strive to maintain the highest standards of honesty and integrity. Never take the money or do anything to jeopardize your license," Reed said sternly, making a point to look each and every one of us in our eyes.

"I'm proud of each and every one of you," Dr. Tuckson said, ending his comments and sealing our covenant.

It sounded like a warning of so many cautionary tales that he'd witnessed during his storied career, mistakes that our university president did not want us to repeat. There was insight in the words that I wouldn't appreciate for years to come. Still, I knew at that time I was hearing something profoundly relevant.

PART 5
MISSION-
DRIVEN

22 | Comeback

"Your order please, sir," my server said. I was so deep in thought I didn't even notice her approach my table.

"Oh, sorry, uh, I'll have broccoli and chicken with brown rice," I replied. It was my usual order from Café Evergreen, my favorite Chinese restaurant on the Upper Eastside. I had it delivered to my apartment countless nights. But on that night, I needed to be out of the apartment. There were things that I needed to sort out. It was time for me to plot my comeback strategy. As I nibbled at my food, I began to ponder how, after spending the previous four years in school becoming a physician, I had come to this fork in the road. If I failed at medicine, what then? There really was no backup plan because I never planned on failing.

Only one month earlier, I was on top of the world as I delivered the student keynote speech at the Drew medical school graduation banquet, received the Most Inspirational Student Doctor award, and won one of only two gold medals awarded at Drew. During the Hippocratic oath ceremony at UCLA's Westwood campus a few days later, I wore shorts, a V-neck T-shirt, and white sneakers under my velvet-striped robe. Too cool for school, I waited on the side of the stage for the dean to read off my accolades, which included the Charles O'Malley bronze medal, the highest honor given for the thesis program at the UCLA School of Medicine. After shaking his hand and posing for a photo, I left the stage. It was a proud day for my family and me.

Reflecting on how far I had come, by the time I finished my broccoli and chicken, I knew I had to stay in the program and stick it out if I could. It was dark outside when I left the restaurant and headed back to my high-rise tower. The air was warm and stale from exhaust fumes mixed with the scent of garbage that lined the streets. *New York. You won't chew me up and spit me out,* I thought, remembering the countless hurdles I had overcome to make it there. *I've come too far to go back now.*

My shrink's name was Dr. Snyder. Seeing him was a requirement to resume my training at the New York Hospital. It stood to reason that the hospital had to protect itself from any liability that I might cause. My comment about making a mistake and possibly hurting a patient wasn't taken lightly. In a weird way, I actually welcomed a chance to lay my burdens on someone else's shoulders. After waiting outside of closed doors for some time, I was eventually escorted into the office, passing a distraught-looking woman exiting. Dr. Snyder was old. Thin and ordinary, with a pasty complexion, a wiry white beard, and round-rimmed glasses, he was nearly buried behind his cluttered desk. With certificates and degrees nailed to the wall above his head, he spoke with a soft voice.

"I'm Doctor Snyder," he said.

"Hi. LaMar Hasbrouck," I replied as I braced for his analytic mind probing.

"How are you feeling?" he asked.

"I'm good, real good," I lied.

"How have you spent your time away from the hospital?" he continued.

"I was able to furnish my apartment and get some rest," I said.

He asked, "Are you feeling ready to return?"

"Yeah. I'm ready," I told him. I wasn't going to say that I wasn't.

"Do you feel like you might hurt yourself or someone else?" he probed.

Laughing, I responded, "No. No, I'm good. I was just a little stressed. I had to get some things in order. I'm okay now. Really, I'm good."

We talked all of about twenty minutes. Much to my amazement, it turned out to be a painless series of rather benign questions. It felt more like a curbside chat than a psychiatric evaluation. He scribbled a few notes, and I was free to go. The session was more of a formality, I figured, because no real counseling took place. *Maybe I didn't really need counseling,* I told myself as I left his office.

When I returned to the hospital's step-down service, a place designated for patients too sick to be on the regular floor but not quite sick enough to require the ICU, I felt better prepared to face my demons and duties. They paired me with a second-year resident named Brian who was a native New Yorker through and through. He was four inches shorter than me, and I stood at just under five ten. Being a short Jewish kid, I wondered if Brian had been an underdog most of his life. From Hicksville, Long Island, he had a working-class likeability about him. We got along fine. We worked together to manage patients that occupied twenty beds, many of whom had been bedridden for months. Most were on ventilators. While there, I learned how to analyze breathing parameters, blood gases, and ventilator settings like PEEP, SIMV, CPAP, and other acronyms that have little meaning outside of the hospital setting.

The work in the step-down unit was steady, but the days ended promptly by five every day. There was no call and no weekend duty. Brian left me alone to manage, sometimes for hours, when he went to lunch conferences or meetings. By writing daily notes summarizing the patient's status in the charts and orders for the nurses to pick up, I grew more confident in my role as a young doctor. When my two weeks on the step-down unit ended, I returned to the towers, the same wards that had broken my spirit and nearly broke me in the process a few weeks earlier. Yet I had a new determination the second time around. After five straight weeks on that rotation, performing scud duties and managing a dozen patients, I moved on to the next service.

As an intern, I rotated through all of the medical services, spending time on the AIDS ward, the neurology unit, and in the ER. I worked the ICU, the cardiac care unit, and on the cancer service. Rotations even included time spent in the world-famous Memorial Sloan-Kettering Cancer Center and the Hospital for Special Surgery. As time went by, I convinced myself that I belonged, and that made life as low man on the totem pole sufferable.

There were times nearly every day when I felt totally outclassed, but performing procedures was not one of them. When it came to doing procedures, I shined like a freshly minted silver dollar. Those Ivy League kids couldn't compete with me in that department. Fearless, I would slide a tube down a patient's throat in a heartbeat. In an emergency situation, with a patient's throat swelling shut, that kind of speed and accuracy was needed. My colleagues looked on with surprise. They didn't realize that having been trained at the King-Drew Medical Center, medical students had to get down and dirty. Some of my former classmates had singlehandedly delivered thirty or more babies during a four-week obstetrics rotation. Because of my Los Angeles County experience, I had plenty of practice performing procedures. Unfortunately, when it came to other aspects of doctoring, I was behind. As fate would have it, the remedial training I needed came in large part from two strong black women in the program. There were only three minority second-year residents out of forty. It just so happened that over the course of my first year, I was paired with two of them.

Cynthia was from Guyana. She had golden brown skin with hair to match. She did her medical schooling in Upstate New York. She had a realness about her that made her approachable. She patiently helped me to fill in the blanks of my knowledge without making me feel small or self-conscious about my ignorance. It was liberating to learn medicine from someone who only demanded that I be willing to learn. She and I talked about our struggles in the program. Amid the busy work, we'd discuss life, training, and family responsibilities. Sometimes it seemed like we were trying to best each other with stories about our challenges and personal miseries.

"Your blues ain't my blues," she'd say. It wasn't hard to see the truth in that statement. Together we took care of patients who had blues that far outweighed hers and mine combined.

Sheila, my other guide and mentor, had a different style altogether. She studied at Notre Dame and the University of Michigan. Her self-confidence was almost intimidating. With dark cocoa-colored skin, her thick, jet-black, shoulder-length hair shone like satin. She wore scrubs, clogs, and a crisp white jacket with few, if any, reference books in her pockets, giving an air that she kept all the knowledge she needed in her head. She wore Coke-bottle thick glasses that detracted from her pleasant looks, masquerading her more as a nerd than the attractive woman she was.

Sheila and I worked on the unit where patients with recent mild heart attacks or unstable chest pain were sent for twenty-four-hour monitoring. On this service, each morning began with the on-call resident reviewing the patient board, discussing the patients on the ward and the work plans for the day. When Sheila ran the board, she did so with complete authority. She never seemed to squirm when asked a question by an attending physician. I never saw her get pimped, although many tried her. She had quick answers and never lost her composure. She gave them white boys a run for their money. After a while, they stopped trying her.

Both Cynthia and Sheila taught me invaluable lessons for surviving the program. One taught me that I could be vulnerable, let my guard down, and ask if I didn't know something. The other taught me that once firm in my knowledge, I shouldn't be afraid to go toe-to-toe with any challenger, no matter how senior. Both women mentored me by example. They made it through their internship and were thriving as second-year residents. They went about their work with their heads held high, like they belonged. As I grew more confident, I tried my best to emulate them, hoping their success would follow.

23 | Call

Even with great mentors, building confidence was difficult as an intern. As the lowest-paid member of the medical team, I was more valued for the tasks that I performed, including bedside procedures, than for my opinions on medical management or diagnoses. The grief that I experienced from residents, supervising physicians, and even patients themselves made it seem as though I was always on call because the events of the day followed me home at night and haunted my subconscious.

Aside from the routine pimping, which I grew to accept as a necessary evil, some attending physicians, it seemed, tried to break me in other ways. One attending stood over me, verbally chastising me until I made a minor change in my daily chart notes for one of his patients. He insisted that I change the word prednisone to prednisolone in describing the plan for the patient. Both medications are steroids, but one was more potent than the other. It was an oversight on my part and relatively unimportant because it was written correctly in the orders for the nurse to follow, which meant that the correct medicine would be given to the patient. But I could see that he wanted to demoralize me with everyone in the nurses' station watching. It worked.

My co-intern, another first-year medical resident, was a female born somewhere in Africa, but she had been raised in the United States since elementary school. She wore her hair in locks and happened to be good friends with my ex-girlfriend. During morning rounds, the attending physician, an old southern gentleman, learned where she was born, and an instant love affair began. He was so enamored, if not fascinated, with her that he gave her a pass at every turn. All the pimping was directed at me while he directed a list of curious but medically irrelevant softball questions, mostly about her personal background, to her.

What's with the love fest? There were plenty of African-born brothers and sisters in New York. Besides, she was culturally African American, having grown up in the States from a young age. Her life couldn't have been more challenging than mine growing up on G Street, surviving on powdered eggs and government cheese. Africa didn't have a market on poverty. In fact, her father was a physician, and her mother an attorney. *Yeah, real tough life,* I thought. This old man was so in awe of her story he couldn't care less about my black behind. It seemed that some white folks had romantic views of foreign-born blacks. But when it came to the garden-variety blacks, those like me born right here in the United States, they were not the least bit impressed.

Racial prejudice was pervasive during my time at the New York Hospital, although some may have chosen to ignore it. My senses picked up everything from the subtlest undercurrents to the overt. During my second year, I experienced a dismissal in front of a room full of my peers that epitomized this behavior.

"Good morning. I'm LaMar. I'm one of the residents," I said. Smiling, I extended my hand toward the attending physician in charge.

It was the morning just after rounds. All four medical teams converged on the conference room for teaching rounds. The group was made up of residents, interns, and medical students. As about sixteen of us got settled in a circle, I stood and walked over to introduce myself to the attending physician before we began to discuss our cases with him. The balding physician in his late forties sat with crossed legs and a crisp, long white coat. He looked me up and down and said nothing as I stood there with my outstretched hand in the air. The room fell silent. His expressionless gaze seemed to look through me, signaling that he had no intention of acknowledging my respectful gesture or me. I felt like Billy Dee Williams in the popular scene in the movie *Lady Sings the Blues* when he states, "Are you just gonna let my hand fall off?"

After nearly ten seconds of deafening silence, I retracted my arm and sat down. After I sat down, he promptly proceeded to introduce himself to the group and then began talking about diseases of the kidney as if my interaction with him had never occurred. After being reduced to an invisible man, it was hard for me to concentrate. *Okay, what just happened?* I was nearly tempted to examine my hand, front and back, for traces of marmalade jelly or dirt. *What did I do wrong?* Certainly as a second-year resident and leader of one of the four on-call medical teams, it was appropriate to introduce myself. *What a pompous A-hole,* I thought as I inspected him closely. After more than an hour of soul searching, I came to the conclusion that I had done nothing wrong.

Being treated like secondhand help by supervising attending physicians was disheartening, defeating really. But I also encountered bigotry from my patients. During a night on call for the Coronary Care Unit, the nurse paged me to look in on a patient. The patient, a very old white man, had been riding his call button all night and making demands. I had a hunch about whose patient it was, and sure enough, when I rushed into the room and grabbed his chart, my hunch was confirmed. He was a Schuyler special. That was the name that my co-interns and I gave to patients admitted by Dr. Schuyler, a sweet, elderly attending physician who probably should have retired long before I entered the training program. His patients were always complicated. They were the sickest, neediest, and most entitled. Frail elderly people, for the most part, and almost every one of them, it seemed, had one foot in the grave and the other foot on a banana peel. Dr. Schuyler appeared to be either the angel of mercy or the grim reaper.

"Who the hell are you—a nurse? I called for the doctor," Schuyler's patient said with resolute contempt.

He was a frail, pasty, old man with little color in his cheeks. He had fear in his eyes but tried desperately to conceal it with anger.

"Sir, I am the doctor. Now how can I help you?" I replied.

"I, I don't want you. Nurse! I want *my* doctor. Nurse!" he yelled while clutching his chest.

"I'm the doctor on call tonight. Tell me what's going on. Are you having chest pain?" I asked the obvious because he was exhibiting the classic Levine's sign, with his clenched fist held over his chest.

His resolved stiffened. "Where's my doctor? I want my doctor," he demanded, raising his weakened voice as best he could.

Something in me almost felt sorry for him—almost. That instant, I looked down at that scared little man and gave him the sobering truth.

"Listen. I am the *only* doctor on call tonight. So if you want some relief from your pain, you'll let me help you. No one else is here. If not, I'm gonna head back to bed, and I wish you luck." I hung his chart at the foot of his bed as if I was leaving. Of course, I would have never left him.

"Wait," he said in a panicked plea and nodded his head in the affirmative, freeing me to care for him. Pain broke his stubborn spirit.

After doing an EKG, which confirmed the origin of pain but no heart attack, I put a little nitroglycerin paste on his chest, gave him a little oxygen, and he settled right down. His pain went from a nine out of ten to a two out of ten within minutes. Before long, he was pain-free and fast asleep.

My patient probably learned nothing that night. Someone eighty years old with long-held beliefs was undoubtedly resistant to learning new things. Or maybe he learned that prejudice and racial bias can sometimes be the biggest barriers to understanding and healing. Nevertheless, when I returned to my call room, I thanked God for using me as a healer and as a teacher. As I laid my head back against the pillow, I smiled, thinking about how the wonders of medicine had empowered me to relieve the pain of a sickened heart. For the next few hours, I slept peacefully. And thanks to me, so did my patient.

24 | Training Days

Famed R&B duo Nick Ashford and Valerie Simpson, singer Toni Braxton, and newswoman Dianne Sawyer were just a few of the long list of celebrities that passed through the doors of the New York Hospital. When Oscar de la Renta handed me his contact information for a patient that I admitted to the Emergency Department, I stopped dead in my tracks. The face of the fashion icon was not familiar to me, but I instantly recognized his signature. I had seen that signature so many times on my mom's favorite fragrance.

Being at the premier hospital in Manhattan, I'd run into celebrities on a regular basis, in the hallways and corridors, at the bedside visiting loved ones, or in some cases in the beds as patients. Not wanting to appear star-struck, I'd act nonchalant and keep about my business. They may have been artists, entertainers, news anchors, and household names, but they didn't know the first thing about the art of medicine.

Probably my most famous patient was the cable broadcasting giant known for wearing suspenders. During a late night on-call, Mr. King drew my number. It was me that interviewed him and his considerably younger fiancée, his future wife number eight, I believe. At one point, she asked me if she could grab him some food from the corner deli. *This woman doesn't have a clue.* A corned beef sandwich had no role in the immediate recovery of heart pain. The guy was just admitted to the ICU and forbidden from having food of any kind.

After examining him and writing his medical orders, I moved on to my other patients. He settled in, received testing the next morning, and was gone within a week.

Life and death, long hours, and celebrity sightings, such was my life as a medical resident. Bit by bit, week after week, I was becoming more competent as a manager of people and their medical conditions.

"What's your name?" a voice rang out from the shadows. The question came from a patient who wasn't mine. He was an older man lying in bed with sheets pulled up to his neck. Engrossed in the busy work of charting, I hadn't even noticed him.

Almost irritated that he had interrupted my morning rounds, I turned to him quickly and replied, "Doctor Hasbrouck."

"No. That's your title. What's your name?" he asked insistently.

At that moment, I paused and tried to see things from his perspective, lying sick in a cold, lumpy bed, bored out of his mind all day, watching people scuttling about doing busy work. Vulnerable and trapped by his failed health, he probably studied every person that entered into his confined space, searching to make sense of his new reality and longing for some human connection. Who was I to deny him that?

"Sorry, I'm LaMar Hasbrouck." I smiled as I approached his bed.

He extended his hand, and we shook. "Pleased to meet you, LaMar Hasbrouck. My name is Tom. Tom Roberts," he said.

That's when the patient became the teacher, and I became the student. He reminded me of what I already knew: patients are people, not a collection of symptoms, lab tests, and hard-to-pronounce diseases. They didn't belong to one doctor or another. It was our collective responsibility to care for their bodies and nurture their souls. That lesson was something that I would never lose sight of, and it was never more important than when I cared for my favorite patient.

MR. EVANS

Mr. Evans came to the hospital with low back pain that turned out to be prostate cancer that had already spread throughout his body. All I had to offer him was a clearer understanding of his medical condition and the care of his beautiful spirit. Sure, I performed all of the tests and probes confirming his diagnosis, but only God's hand could save him at that late stage of his disease process. He was given medicine to make his blood less sticky and less likely to cause clots in his legs and lungs, but even that conservative medical maneuver proved to be dicey.

"Ouch!" he yelled.

"Sorry, Mr. Evans. I know that this is uncomfortable for you, but I need to put this line in," I replied.

I hated sticking his thigh with that large needle over and over again. He and I had become close during the few weeks that I cared for him. He viewed me as sort of a surrogate son, I think. Or maybe he saw a younger version of himself in me. Whatever the case may have been, I always seemed to be able to put a smile on his face when I came around. So I was every bit as tortured for causing him pain.

Where is that vein? I kept asking myself. *Let's see, NAVEL … nerve, artery, vein, empty space, and lymphatic.* I repeated a pneumonic that helped me remember the vital anatomy located in the crease of his thigh. *The femoral vein is supposed to be right here—*

"Ouch!" cried Mr. Evans.

"Sorry," I said empathetically.

"That's all right, son. You do what you gotta do," he said, grimacing.

Mr. Evans had the patience of a saint. I must have pierced the crease of his thigh four or five times. Each time, I hit the blood vessel, but it was the wrong one. The bright red blood that rapidly filled my syringe was sprouting from the high-pressure femoral artery. What I needed to hit was the low-pressure vein. Blood from a vein is dark, almost blue-black, and doesn't squirt; it oozes.

The bleeding from his artery wouldn't stop because of the blood thinner. As he bled into his leg, I realized that if he continued bleeding into the closed compartment, he would compress his muscles, nerves, and other vessels under his skin. I began to panic, watching his skin tighten and the size of his leg balloon, seeing scowls of pain on his face.

"Nurse!" I shouted. "I need some help to stop this bleeding."

That had never happened to me before, so I didn't know what to do. My focus was to stop the bleeding and prevent my favorite patient from losing his leg or bleeding to death. My supervising resident arrived and called the surgeon on duty. The nurse shut off the blood thinner. The surgeon sewed up his blood vessel that I repeatedly punctured and placed a sandbag on his leg for several hours. Finally, the bleeding stopped. Thank God. By the time early morning rounds began the next day, the long, hard night was written all over Mr. Evans's face. He looked completely wiped out. My visit with him was brief that day, mostly consisting of me standing in the doorway to his room watching him sleep.

Mr. Evans and I had several more bedside chats in the weeks to follow, but not nearly enough for me. We both ignored the fact that his was a terminal condition. Doing so made for lighter visits between us, but it wouldn't forestall the inevitable. On June 15, 1995, Mr. Evans made his transition, leaving behind three adult children and the valuable lesson of forgiveness with me, his adopted son. He died when I was off shift, so I did not get to say my final good-byes. I like to think that he much preferred our usual good-byes, with me squeezing his hand at the end of my shift.

"You hang in there, Mr. Evans, and I'll see you tomorrow," I would say.

"All right then, son. Don't forget about me," he'd reply, trying with all his might to proffer a smile.

HEADSTRONG

There is a subtle dress code in hospitals that most visitors do not bother to notice. While the white lab coats worn by hospital types may appear to be the same, they are not. Some are long. Some are short.

Those worn by the attending physicians, the more senior doctors that have completed their residency training, are long. Those white coats worn by resident physicians still in the process of completing their training, like me at the time, are short. I always thought of it as symbolic of having your backside covered versus having your ass exposed.

The short coat, long coat thing is not the routine for all training programs, but at a fairly elitist place like the New York Hospital, it was protocol. Simply put, short coats usually had to get the final sign-off from long coats when it came to the big decisions for a patient's care. When I entered into my senior year of residency, I was determined not to be pushed around by anyone, regardless of the length of my coat. All of that pimping nonsense was behind me. Or at least that's what I hoped. After earning my stripes and taking my bruises, I had achieved the rank of senior resident. It didn't make my coat any longer, but I did feel confident in my ability to lead a team and be an effective medical resident. *You got this, LaMar. This year is your year. Let's finish strong,* I reminded myself almost daily during my third year of training.

Right around this time of my personal awakening, Holly, the chief resident who had my back during my tough patch as an intern, sent an encouraging memo to all interns and residents that confirmed what I intuitively knew. The memo included graphs showing the levels of depression, anxiety, confidence, and satisfaction reported by medical interns and residents over the course of their three years of training. Not surprisingly, anxiety and depression declined sharply after about a year of training. Confidence and job satisfaction, on the other hand, increased by year two and peaked during the last half of the senior year.

My upward trajectory in confidence was unshakable. My job satisfaction was jeopardized only by those who would try to test me. As far as patients went, I understood that pushiness, rudeness, and even racial bigotry were all amplified under the influence of illness. I didn't like it, but I understood and tried not to take it personally. But when it came to my fellow residents, those that wore a short white lab coat similar to mine, I had little tolerance for arrogance.

"I'm not taking this guy up. I'm not impressed, and his first enzyme was normal," David said dismissively.

David was a senior resident in my class. Like all of us, he didn't want to add another patient to his growing list if it could be avoided. He had received a call minutes earlier from me, alerting him that I had someone for him to admit. He was on call for the cardiac observation wards. I was on call in the ER.

"Excuse me?" I replied.

"You heard me. I'm not taking this guy. This presentation looks like a soft rule out. I doubt that he's having an MI," he reasoned.

The term MI is short for myocardial infarction, the medical term for a heart attack. In my clinical opinion, my patient, soon to be David's patient if I had anything to do with it, was having a heart attack.

I responded, "Are you next in line for an admission?"

"Yes," he replied.

"Well, then you are taking this patient," I said.

Confident that my patient had at least two out of the three criteria suspicious for a heart attack, I pressed the issue. The patient had a compelling story in the way he described his chest pain and other symptoms, not to mention having a family history of heart disease, and he had a characteristically abnormal EKG. He lacked an initial positive blood test for heart damage, considered to be the clincher for the diagnosis. But sometimes that test wouldn't show positive for six to twelve hours.

"Look," he said while pointing to the EKG tracing, "these elevations here are minimal."

My classmate continued making his case about how unimpressed he was with the heart tracing. His voice became loud. Judging by the color of his face, his frustration was bordering on anger. Our differing clinical opinions had led to a battle of wills. Now with egos involved, his intern and my intern watched the verbal sparring between us as our intellectual contest disintegrated into a pissing contest between two senior residents.

"The guy's got a convincing story, a positive family history, and an abnormal EKG. If you don't admit him, then we can get the chief resident on the phone and arrange to admit him to another resident, but I'm not sending this patient home. Let me know what you decide. I have to get back to work." I then calmly walked away to assess a new patient that had arrived during our heated debate.

"This is BS!" David said to his intern. "Come on. Let's wheel this guy up."

Twenty minutes later, David, his intern, and the patient had disappeared. Before my twelve-hour shift ended, I made a point to check the lab test for that patient. Sure enough, the second blood test confirmed that the patient had heart damage at a minimum and possibly a heart attack. The patient's story carried the day. My insistence to err on the side of caution was sweetly vindicated.

CIMA

Cornell Internal Medicine Associates (CIMA) was the outpatient practice. Every resident was required to see a panel of patients every week. Dr. Cohn was the long coat assigned to supervise me during my weekly clinic. She was disagreeable and persnickety even when she didn't have to be. If I suggested drug A, she wanted to go with drug B. If I wanted to order lab test X, she preferred test Y.

I could tolerate the occasional pomposity on a one-off basis. The kidney specialist that refused to shake my hand was like that. The attending physician that forced me to change the name of the steroid in my daily progress note treated me like that too. These encounters rubbed me the wrong way, but because they were short-lived, I learned to brush them off. My encounters with Dr. Cohn, on the other hand, endured for years.

As a short coat, I respectfully followed her direction during the first year. As a newbie, I guess that I was too green to question her wisdom. But when I matured as a doctor, I began to grow tired of her all-knowing ways and the manner in which she delivered her advice. *Does she always have to be right? When do I get to make an educated treatment decision?* As the months went by, I had more and more questions. It was apparent that the relationship was anything but mentoring. Suddenly I began to have flashbacks of my days at Berkeley dealing with my instructor for remedial English. Something had to be done.

Sitting back in her chair, slightly rocking, she'd stare at me with all of the arrogance of Hippocrates, the father of Western medicine, each time I presented a patient encounters.

"Go ahead, let's hear about the patient," she'd say, almost dismissively. It irked me like fingernails across a classroom blackboard.

Dr. Cohn never eased up. My respectful pushing back to challenge her opinions did little to remedy the situation. Finally, after two frustrating years, I went to her boss and requested a change. After being reassigned to a new long coat supervisor, I had smooth sailing. Imagine that. It turned out that I did know a thing or two about a thing or two. Months later, my value was reinforced during a routine visit by a patient in the medical clinic.

LIKE JOE LOUIS

"I'm proud of you," my patient said, almost out of the blue. Her salt-and-pepper Afro swayed back and forth as she hurriedly gathered up her things to leave me. I was so preoccupied with moving things along, thinking of ways to save time between her and my next patient, I almost missed it.

"Like Joe Louis. You probably don't remember him," she continued. "When he came back from winning that big fight, we were all so proud of him. That's how I feel. You're young and black and a doctor."

I stopped and smiled and thanked her. *Who else could she have given those kind words to in this clinic? Sadly few,* I thought. Still my heart was happy, happy to be me.

My encounter with that black woman who could have been my

grandmother made me feel special. Being made to feel special during medical training happened rarely. Sometimes it felt like I had nothing but bad days and worse than bad days. Feeling underappreciated and overwhelmed was the rule, not the exception. If I were lucky, I might get an occasional word of praise from a nurse or supervising physician. But this was different. Here I was being appreciated for simply being me, or maybe for having the courage to maintain my self-identity.

I never saw that old woman again. I lost the patient, but I retained the lesson. Lessons sometimes seem to stick better when they are put to you by your own folk. The real significance of our meeting was the fact that we represented two different places in history. She represented the past, and I embodied the future. The fact that we both endured the racial discrimination of our time did not diminish our mutual appreciation for the progress we made as a people.

25 | Legacy

Minority residents in the New York Hospital medicine program were sparse. Minority faculty members were rarer still. But there was a critical mass of minority trainees if you combined the minorities from each of the three classes. There was a total of nine: one African American in the senior class, three in the junior class, and four blacks and one Puerto Rican in my class. We got organized and banded together to relay our unique issues to the department leadership.

We called ourselves the Minority House Staff Committee, MHC for short, and I was elected as the first chairman. We were recognized by the residency director, Dr. Mark Pecker, and sponsored by the ranking African American faculty member, Dr. Carol Storey-Johnson. We were even given official letterhead and assigned administrative support. We were legitimized as an official committee for the medical program.

Our meetings took place in my studio apartment in the Helmsley Medical Tower overlooking the East River. We sat for hours on my lumpy futon and a few hard bar stools as I banged out our mission statement on my Macintosh Apple computer, a gift from the late baseball hall of famer Tony Gwynn and his wife. Our mission was simple. We wanted to actively recruit and retain more residents of color and support them through the program. We wanted minority trainees to thrive, not just limp through the program battered and bruised.

In just one short year, our outreach paid off. The complexion of incoming classes began to change. What started as the collective will of nine had matured into a program-wide imperative. For our efforts, we received the David B. Skinner Award for administrative stewardship, a prestigious honor named after the pioneering physician who led the merger of the New York Hospital with the Columbia Presbyterian Hospital to form the largest academic medical center in the country, New York-Presbyterian Hospital.

At the time of this writing, the MHC is in its twentieth year, with an active membership of twenty-one residents. According to the website description, the MHC "works to increase the number of underrepresented minorities ... through a variety of projects including outreach activities, networking events with staff and medical students, and volunteerism in the community." In other words, the mission conceived on my futon so many years ago lives on today.

The other legacy that I had hoped to leave was one of scholarship. The work I completed after spending three months in Brazil, researching an infectious disease that primarily affected poor people living in the lowlands, was selected as a finalist in the David E. Rogers Memorial Research Competition. I desperately wanted my name etched into a plate on that perpetual plaque. After a lot of preparation and rehearsal, my PowerPoint slide deck showed the slum conditions of Salvador, Bahia, yellow-eyed, sick patients with failing livers, and charts and graphs showing the factors that predict death for infected patients. I stepped up to the podium wearing suspenders, a bowtie, and my short white coat, doing my best to look the part of a distinguished physician. I gave a strong presentation and successfully fielded nearly a dozen questions from interested faculty seated in the audience. And judging from the response of the audience, my performance was stellar.

Sitting back, I watched my fellow residents give their talks in turn. One did a good job. One fumbled through his presentation so badly it was uncomfortable. The remaining finalist struggled so much during the question-and-answer period that his faculty preceptor jumped up to put him out of his misery. It was painful to watch. There was no question in my mind that I had surpassed them all. So, as I waited with the others for the five faculty judges to tally their scores, I felt confident but oddly uneasy. You know, almost like things seemed too good to be true.

When the chief resident, Holly, approached the podium to announce the winner, my heart felt like it was skipping rope.

"And the winner is … *not LaMar.*" Of course, she didn't say that, but that's essentially what I heard.

Wow. Are you kidding me, Holly? How could that be?

I'll get runner-up for sure. Nope. That honor went to my bumbling classmate who was saved by his faculty preceptor. Something was wrong. Later that day, at least half a dozen of my classmates and one of the attending physicians who sponsored a finalist told me that I was flat-out robbed. Holly, who had voted herself, told me that she was surprised.

"I don't know what happened. I gave you a five out of five," she confided to me.

With that feedback and my search for justice, I racked my brain the entire day trying to figure out what went wrong. Finally, as if struck by lightning, I figured out who had sabotaged me. Just a day before the competition, I had stopped by the office of the chair for the General Medicine Fellowship program to tell her that I was declining her offer to enter the program.

"She's out of the office, Doctor. Have you decided? Are you going to take it?" her assistant asked. "You can tell me. I won't say a word."

Against my better judgment, I reluctantly told her my decision.

"No. I don't think I'm going to take it," I said.

She assured me that she would let me tell her boss myself, but I know that didn't happen. The assistant probably had her boss on the phone before I made it into the elevator. The next day, judging from her lack of eye contact with me, there was hell for me to pay. She probably bottomed out my scores on purpose. I should have just kept my big mouth shut, at least until after the competition.

As a result, the prize in research eluded me. But the legacy of supporting more than a hundred minority students through one of the most highly regarded medicine residency programs on the East Coast shines brighter than my name on some small gold plate fastened to a plank of wood.

26 | Two Cents

Anticlimactic. That is the best way to describe finishing my residency training. There was no graduation, no fanfare. There was an end-of-the-year banquet, but I didn't see any reason for me to attend. Having been screwed in the research competition, I suppose that I was still a little bitter. Besides, as a newlywed and father of a six-month-old daughter, I was busy planning my wedding ceremony for the family that was to take place in Southern California. My priorities were to make sure that I had my wall certificate as proof of completing the training program and passing my board exams. My grandfather, Poppa, told me after my medical school graduation that the world was my oyster. So I was anxious to go out into the vast unknown and make my mark.

Harvard was my next stop. So I thought. The program that I thought was so perfect for me, the Commonwealth Fellowship in Minority Health Policy, rejected me. Because the fellowship awarded a master's degree in public health, a degree I had previously earned at Berkeley, I was deemed ineligible. It was hard for me to believe that I was overqualified for a Harvard learning opportunity, but apparently I was. The take-home lesson for me was that timing was as important as merit, sometimes even more important. Rejected by Harvard's school of public health, I was forced to consider other possibilities.

Joining a private or group medical practice, pursuing more training, taking a faculty position at the university or a government job, living on the East Coast or the West Coast, I had some quick thinking to do. In the end, I relocated my young family to the new South, choosing an academic position as a clinical assistant professor at the Emory University School of Medicine in Atlanta, Georgia.

"No. No way. I don't want anybody trying to experiment on me. I know how it works. You're just trying to get more money, probably in bed with the drug companies. No way." Mr. Taylor was adamant in refusing his screening exam.

"Mr. Taylor, this is a screening test that we recommend to everyone over age fifty. It's considered standard. It will allow us to check for early signs of colon cancer," I tried to explain.

He wasn't buying it. "Yeah, right," he said. "And who are you anyway?"

His reply struck me as odd because I had introduced myself just minutes earlier when I entered the examination room. But I soon learned that he was getting at something altogether different.

"I'm Doctor Hasbrouck."

"No, I mean, are you with Morehouse or Emory?" he replied.

Immediately, I understood what he was insinuating. Because the clinic was located within the Grady Memorial Hospital building, a hospital shared by both Morehouse, a historically black medical school, and Emory, a white institution, he naturally assumed that because I was black I was affiliated with Morehouse.

"Well, what difference does it make, Mr. Taylor?" I inquired.

"Well, because my doctor here is with Emory," he proudly replied as he pointed to the white resident physician that he had come to know as his doctor. Meanwhile, the doctor wearing the short coat was noticeably uncomfortable, so much so that his face was turning beet red.

"Well, Mr. Taylor, I happen to be the *supervising* physician at Emory. That's why I'm here, to supervise your doctor and make sure that he does not miss anything," I continued. His face nearly hit the floor.

"Oh, okay. But I'm still not gonna get that test," he said, defiantly turning back to the resident, refusing to let go of his belief that he would be provided superior care by a white doctor wearing a short coat than a black doctor wearing a long one.

"That is your choice. I just want to make sure that we offer the test to you and that you understand why we recommend it," I explained.

"Yeah, yeah, yeah ... well, I ain't getting it." He rudely cut me off.

At that point, I instructed the resident to document in the medical chart that the patient refused the test, wished Mr. Taylor well, and went on about my day. It was a common case of ignorance. It was also a reflection of just how much some of us black folk continued to buy into the myth of black inferiority. How else would you explain why he readily assumed that I was the junior physician affiliated with what was in his mind the inferior black institution? He probably assumed that I was being supervised by his white doctor, rather than the other way around. Like a broken record, I witnessed the phenomenon of people underestimating the intellect and competence of minority physicians. Sadly, over time I almost came to expect it.

TOUGH LOVE

"Doctor Hasbrouck, is there anything that I can do? I'd be willing to do extra credit or spend another week on the wards," the medical student pleaded to me, almost in a panic.

"I don't think so," I replied calmly.

It wasn't that I was unsympathetic, but it didn't seem appropriate that the student would assume a passing grade for the medicine rotation I led simply because he showed up. Perhaps it was part of a culture of entitlement that was so common. Nevertheless, I had a habit of being fair. If you didn't do the work, you weren't going to pass. My policy was as simple as that.

Often late and seldom interested in the topic of the day, this particular student, who happened to be white, went through the motions week after week. His engagement and overall performance were piss-poor. He came and went as he pleased. Seemed like every other day I was making a mental note of his unprofessional behavior. Occasionally, I would counsel him but to no avail. He was determined to do things his way and on his timeline. To add insult to injury, he had the nerve to skip the last three days of the four-week rotation to start his vacation early.

"But, Doctor Hasbrouck, I really learned a lot on your rotation. I don't understand," he said.

Call it a lack of academic intuition or an air of superiority, but surprisingly the student was shocked to learn that he had not earned a passing grade. It was too late for him to brown-nose on the back end. His pleading fell on deaf ears. In the end, the course director took pity on him, and he was required to repeat only half of the rotation, undoubtedly a welcome relief for the student and far more generous than I would have been. For me, however, his light punishment reinforced what I was beginning to recognize as a universal principal: some people always seemed to be given the benefit of the doubt, while others could never seem to catch a break. In my experience, justice was relative. It often depended on who you knew and the color of your skin, something I called the politics of pedigree and privilege.

Whether it was an elderly black woman who refused a mammogram arguing, "If God gon' take me from cancer, He just gon' have to take me," or the Indian gentleman continuing to sneak cigarettes after having suffered his second stroke, or men like Mr. Taylor who refused their screening colonoscopy because he thought I was trying to experiment on him, I discovered the health literacy and compliance of some people left much to be desired. For that reason, I was determined to educate even my most stubborn patients. The way I looked at it, every patient encounter was a fresh opportunity to care for and support someone in their quest to extend their length and quality of life. Part teacher, part doctor, part stereotype-buster, I figured that the best way to maximize my contributions to improving the health of vulnerable people was to choose my career opportunities wisely. If I was going to make my two cents count, I had to be strategic in the way I chose to give back.

27 | Secret

Throughout my uncertain journey, I have discovered the simple secret for success. It boils down to being four things, principles that I call the "four bes": be you, be audacious, be passionate, and be humble. Let me explain.

BE YOU

The most important principle is *be you*. I have certainly been challenged in this area on more than a few occasions. I will share two examples with you. The first one relates to an experience that allowed me to embrace more fully my blackness. You see, in the early eighties when I attended college, relaxed hair was in style. Brothers who were tired of greasy Jerry curls opted instead to perm (or chemically process) their hair. You could do it yourself by simply combing the cream product through your hair and then washing it out. I relaxed my hair plenty of times without incident. However, apparently on this particular occasion, I had gotten hold of a bad jar.

When I went to rinse the cream out of my hair, my hair rinsed out with it! Horrified to see my hair circling the drain, and in terrible pain from the spray of the shower beating down on my scalp, I vowed that I would never chemically treat my hair again. Weeks later, after the second-degree burns to my scalp healed and the scabs fell off, I went to a local barbershop and had my hair shaved off.

After a few months, my head was full of the wool that God

gave me. During the next year, I grew my hair into twists called micro-locks, an Afrocentric hairstyle. Something that had begun as a traumatic experience evolved into a process of self-discovery. Ironically, just as I was becoming more comfortable being me, I was faced with a potential uncertainty.

The year was 1989. I began to prepare to apply to medical schools. The dilemma was, should I interview for medical school as an outwardly self-aware black man, or should I cut my locks off to conform? Friends and fellow students warned me against appearing too radical. As if my blackness was an affront to the establishment. As if wearing my hair in a culturally expressive way would be objectionable to the gatekeepers for the medical profession. "Are you going to wear your hair like *that* for your interviews?" they asked. The suggestion was that I strongly reconsider.

But I had no intention of changing my appearance. I felt strong. After all, it was my academic performance that earned me the right to interview for medical schools in the first place. I decided that medical schools would simply have to take me as is, locks and all.

In every instance when I have encountered someone attempting to be someone that they are not, it has resulted in miserable failure. Admittedly, during my evolution as a person, I have had fleeting thoughts of perpetrating a fraud, but I could never bring myself to take on a phantom identity. The way I figured it, if I were not comfortable in my skin, I would have a more difficult time trying to assume someone else's identity. The real me is better than the fake someone else any day.

I believe that people with a clear sense of who they are have the best chances to achieve their goals. The road to success is riddled with potholes and unexpected detours. Having self-knowledge is like riding on a new set of tires. Road conditions may be uncertain, but you remain firmly grounded as you swerve in and out of the hazardous terrain, avoiding most of the obstacles. Having a sense of community and the knowledge of history will anchor you through turbulent times that are certain to come.

BE AUDACIOUS

The second principle for success is to be audacious. Be bold in your goal setting and in your approach to achieving your goals. Nelson Mandela, the great South African freedom fighter, gave a speech during his presidential inauguration in 1994 in which he recited the writings of Marianne Williamson. I have a portion of this speech posted on the wall in my office:

> Our deepest fear is not that we are inadequate.
> Our deepest fear is that we are powerful beyond measure.
> It is our light, not our darkness that frightens us.
> We ask ourselves, who am I to be brilliant ... and talented?
> Actually, who are you not to be?
> You are a child of God.
> Your playing small doesn't serve the world.
> There's nothing enlightened about shrinking so that other people won't feel insecure around you.
> We were born to make manifest the glory of God that is within us.
> It is not just in some of us. It is in everyone.
> And as we let our light shine, we unconsciously give other people permission to do the same.
> As we are liberated from our fears, our presence automatically liberates others.

When I speak to young people, I often introduce the *be audacious* concept by asking the question: Why not you? "Why can't it be you that discovers the cure for cancer or AIDS?" I ask. "Why can't it be you that invents or improves upon a product that will revolutionize the way we perform some vital task?" I ask. The idea is to be bold in choosing short- and long-term goals for yourself. If you are going to be a dreamer, dream large.

Question: how does a relative nobody in high school sports go on to become a captain for a Division I NCAA football team that competes in a conference with University of Southern California, Stanford, UCLA, Oregon, to name a few? The answer: audacious thinking. A journey that began with an audacious dream led me into fierce PAC-10 competition on the plush fields of magnificent coliseums like the Rose Bowl Stadium in Pasadena, California, and ended at the head table during the senior banquet for the Cal Football team.

BE PASSIONATE

The third principle for success is to be passionate. The word *passion* is defined as "boundless enthusiasm." I feel passionate about teaching, for example. I love to turn the light on for others, and I love to share knowledge. I believe that all knowledge is gained for the purpose of sharing it with others. As the African proverb goes, "He who learns teaches."

I am sure that it was my passion for teaching that led to one of my most memorable teaching opportunities to date. I was invited to address the entire student body of Morehouse College on October 24, 2002, during a mandatory assembly called Crown Forum. This formal event provides students with the opportunity to hear from national thought leaders and noted authorities that lecture on many important topics. Speakers discuss ethical issues, timely world events, and other subjects important for character development. Such high ideas are essential for helping students shape their views of the world. The talks inspire students to lead ethical and civic-minded lives.

Martin Luther King Jr., the most famous graduate of Morehouse College, once said, "Intelligence plus character—that is the goal of a true education." Crown Forum is an important part of that true educational process at Morehouse. It is a necessary part of a student's journey and deemed essential for the transition from men of Morehouse to "Morehouse Men."

I was asked to give a talk at Crown Forum about AIDS. In years past, they had pep rallies for the Crown Forum assembly during homecoming week. This year, students wanted a speaker to discuss a serious health issue. My concern, however, was that this was a pretty sobering topic to discuss during such a festive week of activities.

Smack in the middle of a week filled with concerts, rallies, rap sessions, fraternity and sorority step shows, the big football game on Saturday against Lane College, famous alumni visits to campus, and the coronation ball, they wanted me to talk about AIDS. In essence, they wanted me to speak to men at the prime of their youth during one of the most memorable times in their college experience about a life-threatening disease. Not very festive, but that is what they wanted.

Because it was an opportunity to teach, my enthusiasm remained at a high level. So much so that my excitement bubbled over, and I told a colleague at work about the opportunity. She sharply warned me that there would be nothing that I could say to this group of young men that would change their behavior. "You don't have AIDS. You can't tell them what it's like to live with the disease," she said. "Besides," she continued, "if they don't know how to protect themselves by now, they'll never get it. What could you possibly tell them in thirty minutes that would make them want to change their ways?"

Undeterred, I called my mentor, Reed, for encouragement. After talking with him, I put together a message that I hoped might hit the mark. I did not aim to change their behavior. My goal was simply to move them to a point where they would evaluate their risk more carefully. Prepared to tell them that they had no business jeopardizing their future as leaders by making bad decisions that could prematurely end their lives, I planned to give them the facts about AIDS and not hold anything back. Most importantly, I planned to impart this knowledge with the love of a big brother.

When the day of the talk came, I drove onto the campus with script in hand, practicing my talk out loud on the drive over. I approached the guard tower at the entrance to the campus with nervous anticipation. I told the campus police officer my name and waited. She spoke into her handheld radio. "I have the speaker for Crown Forum, Doctor Hasbrouck, here at the entrance. I'm sending him your way." Turning to me, she said, "Okay, Doctor, you can go."

I drove onto the campus to the historic Martin Luther King Jr. International Chapel. It was only half a block from the guard booth, but I took my time. The hustle and bustle of college life was delightful in its spectacle. Seeing young black students crisscrossing the yard on their way to or from class made me long for my college days. When I made it to the chapel, I was greeted by another police officer who removed a barricade and directed me to my reserved parking space, just beside the church entrance. There, a student met my car and escorted me into a small study within the building. I joined others who would take the platform with me that morning. I exchanged niceties with all present and then began to look over my notes.

As I tried to focus on my talk, I couldn't resist the urge to soak up the history surrounding me. The small library contained shelves packed with countless volumes of literary works. Archival photographs adorned every wall from top to bottom. Many of the photos were black and whites of Martin Luther King Jr. Others documented the legacy of other important people, organizations, and social movements. I was awestruck, smiling inwardly from ear to ear because I was about to be added to the list of men and women to take center stage on this prestigious platform.

Minutes after I arrived, our procession would begin. Under the critical eye of the deans, we took pains to set the exact order in which we were to walk onto the stage so that I would end up in the center seat on the platform. And as the more than twenty-person procession walked onto the stage, I extended to my tallest height, my head held high, my shoulders back. After the preliminary speakers and a musical selection, I was introduced. I rose, buttoned my jacket, and walked calmly to the podium. I took off my glasses and looked out over the podium and into the faces of more than two thousand young men. And then I gave that talk.

A few weeks later, I received a call from the dean responsible for coordinating the event. She called to thank me. She went on to tell me that it was her practice to sit at the very back of the room to gauge the level of interest of the students.

"I want you to know, Doctor Hasbrouck, that you commanded

the full attention of the audience. Your talk was riveting, engaging, and informative. I believe that what you said resonated with those young men," she said.

I swelled with gratitude, knowing that my talk was a success and that I had made a small difference. The comments from the dean were confirmation of that. And as I reflected on the entire experience from the invitation to her comments of thanks, I realized that one of my most important credentials had become my boundless enthusiasm. I wasn't as accomplished as past speakers at this prestigious event. But I had passion. My passion and sincerity were the wings that carried me to the podium on that day.

BE HUMBLE

For some, success has a tendency to lead to feelings of undeserved superiority and distasteful pomposity. I have come to know that our personal achievements happen in part because of hard work and tenacity but also as a result of so many things that we have no control over, such as timing, serendipity, and even divine destiny. Therefore, it is important for us to be humble. In my opinion, success for the sake of success, or material possessions, is empty. In many of the most important ways, success is about those outside of us. It is about all the people who might benefit from our personal success, be it our stories, advice, or the opportunities we create, in ways that will enable them, in turn, to realize their human potential. Our legacy will never truly be measured by the amount of stuff we accumulate, the money we stack, the power or influence we wield, or how successful the world may view us. The full measure of our legacy will be the number of lives that we improve or inspire during our life's journey.

Martin Luther King Jr. said, "Not everybody can be famous, but everybody can be great because greatness is determined by service." In my opinion, service requires the spirit of humility. Only when we see ourselves as servants to others (e.g., our families, coworkers, and fellow man) will we realize that while we may never be rich, we can become immensely enriched in ways far greater than material wealth.

If I have been fruitful in my career, it is because I have followed these four simple principles: self-awareness, audacity, passion, and humility. I have never finished at the top of my class in any subject or earned the title best or brightest. But I have consciously made an effort to leverage my education and talents, continually grow my skill sets, and align my efforts with something bigger than myself: the health and longevity of communities, particularly challenged communities. In this way, I have attempted to be my best and brightest.

Afterword

It was the summer of 2000. I had been asked to give a talk to a group of incoming students at Morehouse College in Atlanta, Georgia. I struggled to find my message. For me, speaking is about telling a story. Every storyteller needs to have a hook. I hadn't found one. Nevertheless, it was important to me to make a positive impression on these young men, to try to inspire them to raise their personal bar for achievement. This talk was the kind of opportunity I enjoyed. The opportunity allowed me to help prepare young people for an important life transition. In this case, the transition was from high school to college.

When I stepped into the small theater of the three-story redbrick building to give my remarks, I was met by a room full of seventeen- and eighteen-year-old young black men.

"All right, gentlemen, settle down. I want to introduce you to someone." The heavyset professor and program coordinator called the students to order. The students began to settle down a bit.

"Our speaker today is Doctor Hasbrouck. Please give him your undivided attention. Go ahead, Doc," he said as he turned to me.

"Uh, thank you, Professor," I said. I looked into the faces of members of the so-called endangered species.

Suddenly, I was overtaken by a sense of privilege, personal pride, and almost divine purpose. More than a hundred young men sat in chairs with the small desks that flip up from underneath the armrests..

Some of them had blown-out Afros with picks stuck in them. Some had braids. Some wore their hair in Nubian locks like mine at the time. And some had shaved heads. Most of the young men were dressed traditionally, but a few of the young men sported Afrocentric attire. Some were wearing urban street gear, with baggy pants, boots, and oversized sports jerseys. Each one expressed a unique self-image.

As I looked on, my chest swelled with nervous anticipation. Then, after nearly a minute of silent gazing and fumbling with my notes, I smiled. The hook to my talk came to me in that split second. I decided to begin my remarks by asking a set of questions.

"By a show of hands, how many of you grew up without your father?" I queried the audience.

I raised my hand first. I wanted to put aside all misconceptions that I was an educated brother of privilege, probably a second- or third-generation professional when they heard me introduced as "Doctor Hasbrouck."

I asked my next question. "How many of you grew up on welfare or food stamps?"

I raised my hand again. My series of questions continued. I ran down the list of the usual neighborhood ills, such as alcohol and drug abuse, violence, crime, and uneven school performance.

"By a show of hands, how many of you received failing grades in school or had to repeat a class?" I asked. Along with most of the audience, I raised my hand after every question.

As a result of this honest exercise, in spite of the obvious generational gap, many of the barriers between us vanished almost immediately. Maybe because they saw themselves in me, they were more willing to tune into what I had to say. And because I could see the seventeen-year-old version of myself in them, I understood their skepticism.

They needed to know that I had a deeper understanding of their reality. Most importantly, they needed to know that their bold dreams to defy the odds that predicted they were more likely to end up in prison (or dead) than in college were valid. They beat the odds. They were students entering college. My mission, as I saw it, was to help them understand the power in that.

As these truths sunk in, the slightly curious faces that greeted me at the beginning of my talk transformed. They became animated. The young men sat up a little straighter. They became interested in my message.

The direction in which they were pointed was far more important than where their journey had begun. I was given an opportunity to speak words into the hearts and minds of these young men that could help to fortify their dreams at a crucial moment in their lives. For the entire time spent with the young men, I did my level best to sow seeds into them that, if nurtured over time, would germinate into trees of knowledge, wisdom, ingenuity, authenticity, and boundless possibilities. When I finished sharing, the young men applauded wildly. Some of them even gave me a standing ovation. And virtually every question or comment by the young men began with a genuine expression of gratitude for my sharing.

We, as resilient African American men, continue to create and then latch onto dreams, motivating ourselves to strive for what is larger even than our circumstances. The fact that I was standing in a lecture hall filled with young black men proved that, I thought.

Something very special happened during that ninety-minute lecture. We validated one another: speaker to audience, audience to speaker, students to students. We were men standing shoulder to shoulder, united in a common goal—to maximize our personal and collective potential. Lions.

No one would have predicted that the place where I grew up or the public elementary schools that I attended would produce the man standing before those young men on that day. Because people from my community did not visualize or hope for that kind of a miracle in me, they did not encourage me to pursue lofty goals. Teachers, counselors, neighbors, even my family had no idea of the true worth of that nappy-headed, fatherless little boy.

There must be other young people out there courageously pushing against the grain of low expectations, fighting against the lure of mediocrity—young people growing up poor, perhaps in a single-parent household, eating mayonnaise toast, wearing hand-me-down clothes, imagining a future beyond their circumstances. Maybe all they need is a reassuring word or sign or the chance to happen upon someone's personal story of triumph to motivate them to take the next step toward their destiny.

If others could learn from my story, I thought, *why not?* My choices during childhood and through my early adulthood resulted in just as many failures as successes. Thankfully, I took the time to learn a few important lessons along the way. Positive reactions to my lowlights and life snippets following a keynote lecture, an official hearing, or an informal mentoring session seemed to confirm what I had suspected: tales of hope and determination are universal.

G Street Lion is my way of channeling these lessons—lessons that I now know were a gift from God. My wish is that readers may glean from my account that stereotypes and bigotry need not predict the trajectory of one's life. The path to success requires only optimism and a stubborn belief in oneself.

Epilogue

It is often said that to have a testimony, you must first have a test. My testimony continues to unfold because I am tested on a regular basis. Following residency training, I faced the Goliath of the medical board exam. After two years of self-study, review courses, and three attempts, I finally passed the exam, transitioning from being a board-eligible physician to a board-certified one.

Following one year as a teaching professor at Emory University, I joined the nation's premier health agency, the Centers for Disease Control and Prevention, CDC for short. I was accepted into the Epidemic Intelligence Service (EIS), the CDC's oldest and most selective fellowship for disease detectives. Sometimes called "the CIA of diseases," EIS officers have investigated disease outbreaks, natural and man-made disasters, and other public health emergencies from mercury poisoning to Ebola since 1951. In 1998, I joined this elite group of physicians and scientists and learned how to track down and combat diseases across the nation and around the world.

During my eleven-year stint at the CDC, I had the chance to address some of the most relevant health concerns of our time, including AIDS, smallpox, youth violence, and heart disease. Along the way, I was actively engaged in the two largest global health initiatives in history: polio eradication and the President's Emergency Plan for AIDS Relief. My travels took me to places that I had only read about, from Kingston, Jamaica, to Dhaka,

Bangladesh, to Port-au-Prince, Haiti, to Entebbe, Uganda, and many more. I met heads of state, US ambassadors, health ministers, representatives from major nongovernmental organizations like the Clinton Foundation, World Bank, and the International Monetary Fund, and lots and lots of other smart people. With progressive promotions of responsibility, I was eventually appointed as director of the CDC office in Guyana, South America, where as a part of the US embassy team, I worked directly with the government of Guyana, international partners, and others to reduce the impact of AIDS on this resource-limited country.

During the two years that I was in Guyana, my family traveled on diplomatic passports, regularly attended events at the home of the US ambassador to Guyana, enjoyed the luxuries of being chauffeured in lightly armored vehicles and having a housekeeper and cook, and lived in a massive house overlooking the ocean. My daughters attended the international school and spent their free time playing in the ambassador's pool, walking along the sea wall, and swinging in hammocks while browning in the South American sun. They even joined the national swim team. It was a far cry from my G Street beginnings, to be sure.

Working to improve the health of communities from the thirty-thousand-foot level had its limitations. Not only was the bureaucracy a challenge, but the politics and lack of academic freedom were at times suffocating. Besides that, it was sometimes difficult to appreciate the impact of your efforts. So after spending more than a decade at the CDC, it was time for me to move on. I made a choice to leave the feds and work on the ground, closer to the people.

My job hunting led me to New York State's Hudson Valley region and a job directing a small county health department. A relative big fish in a small pond, my assignment was to transform a department with talented and committed staff but tainted by corruption and inefficiencies into a credible, streamlined, modern-day agency capable of galvanizing partners to work together to improve the health for their nearly two hundred thousand residents.

"How long would you stay?" the county executive's general counsel asked during my interview for the job.

"Likely three to five years," I answered honestly.

I guess it was obvious that a highly credentialed city kid would not spend the remainder of his career in rural Ulster County. Nonetheless, I was confident that I could deliver the goods for the time that I was there. Sure enough, before long, success after success followed. After two years there, I had an opportunity to duplicate these successes in a place that dwarfed Ulster County in population, staff, budget, and responsibility. The executive for New York's richest county of one million residents, Westchester, interviewed me for their health chief opening. It went well, very well. In fact, I was confident that I had won the job. That is until I was summoned to an impromptu meeting with my boss. It didn't feel right from the start.

"So I got a call from the county executive in Westchester," my boss stated.

Oh, boy. Here it comes. I thought about what that conversation must have been.

"Look, I get it," my boss continued. "It's a bigger job. You want to grow. I get it. I support that. I only ask that you come to me first so that I can help you get to the next level."

"Sure. I can do that," I said. Perplexed, I couldn't figure out if his response was an endorsement or a warning.

My conversation with the county executive continued for another ten minutes. We shook hands, and I walked out of his office, still unclear as to what had transpired. Three weeks passed, and I heard nothing from Westchester County. That's when I figured it out. The deal was dead in the water. Nearly two months later, I received a call from the Westchester deputy executive, informing me that they had, in his words, "decided to go in a different direction."

Apparently, it wasn't time for me to move on, not yet. A few months later, another opportunity presented itself; this one even dwarfed the Westchester job. Following several months of vetting and interviews, I was appointed by Governor Pat Quinn as the top health official for the nation's fifth largest state, Illinois, reporting directly to the governor and responsible for leading an agency to protect the health and improve the lives of nearly thirteen million residents. The $600 million budget for my new job was more than the entire budget for the county. Then, after about three years there, an even bigger opportunity, one of national importance, presented itself. It seemed that the universe was stubborn in conspiring to elevate me to my purpose. To paraphrase one of my favorite Bible verses, "my gifts were making room for me" and bringing me before great men.

Notwithstanding my gifts, tests were a necessary part of my journey, and I grew to expect them. They usually came in the form of someone questioning my commitment, competence, or character. Sometimes my loudest cheerleader would sour seemingly overnight, to become my harshest critic. One moment, I was brilliant; the next moment, I was cocky. I was considered an articulate agency spokesperson one minute and then muffled by the master the very next. Was I changing? My scope of influence was broadening, but I wasn't changing at all. Simply put, I was growing without asking permission. And for reasons unknown to me, that made some people uncomfortable.

Few would have predicted that G Street would produce a man so capable of unapologetic growth. And if someone thought it possible to produce such a man, certainly no one would have picked me. Luckily, I became adept at replicating this process of self-development. Along the way, I discovered the secret formula for success.

These guiding principles have taken me from powdered eggs and government cheese to the premier public university in the country. From the run-down dirt fields of the Pop Warner leagues in southeast San Diego to manicured lawns of some of the most storied football coliseums in the country. From Ds and Fs in middle school to a medical degree with honors and to the far corners of the earth on medical missions, allowing me to meet heads of state, stand at podiums side by side with governors, US congressmen, and civil rights icons, and attend invitation-only events at the White House.

Today, I continue to pursue my professional and personal goals like a lion wading through tall grass. Like a lion, I take measured and persistent steps when stalking my goals. With every well-placed stride has come the potential for significant growth. Many of my targets have been opportunities cleverly disguised as insurmountable challenges. In many cases, no one sees me coming.

Printed in the United States
By Bookmasters